T0277411

CRANE LOCOMOTIVES

JOHN WOODHAMS

AMBERLEY

First published 2022

Amberley Publishing
The Hill, Stroud,
Gloucestershire, GL5 4EP

www.amberley-books.com

ISBN: 978 1 3981 0991 9 (print)
ISBN: 978 1 3981 0992 6 (ebook)

British Library Cataloguing in Publication Data.
A catalogue record for this book is available from the British Library.

Typeset in 10pt on 13pt Celeste.
Typesetting by SJmagic DESIGN SERVICES, India.
Printed in the UK.

Contents

Introduction

The first cranes mounted on railway wheels were hand operated, but by the mid-nineteenth century, several builders had fitted steam engines and boilers to enhance lifting capabilities, although initially these machines were not self-propelled, but merely portable. By the 1860s self-propelled, or locomotive cranes, often capable of shunting a wagon or two, were offered and gradually designs were developed for more specialised uses, such as accident cranes or for quarrying. As accident cranes could be required at any point on the railway's network, they also had to be capable of being hauled on the main line, in a train, and hence became known as travelling cranes. As they grew in size and lifting capacity, they became more commonly known as breakdown cranes.

A crane locomotive is essentially a conventional steam locomotive built or converted to carry a crane jib – with the crane operating mechanism entirely independent of propulsion, whereas a locomotive or self-propelled crane utilises the mechanism of the crane itself to transmit power to its wheels, usually either by gearing or chain drive. The Industrial Railway Society has conveniently defined a crane locomotive as having separate cylinders to propel the machine. The term crane locomotive was also applied in the road steam industry, with small numbers of road locomotives built with a crane attachment, usually at the front end. Although not normally described as crane locomotives, showmen's engines too were usually fitted with lifting gear and a detachable jib behind the bunker to assist with the setting up and dismantling of fairgrounds.

A crane locomotive could be used to load and unload adjacent wagons, and its greater mobility thus creates a very versatile machine, particularly for use in sites such as shipyards, steelworks and railway workshops. Cranes were variously mounted centrally over the boiler, at the rear, more or less in the footplate area, and even at the smokebox end attached to the chimney. The largest examples were capable of lifting up to 10 tons, although most were in the 3-to-7-ton range, but designs were always constrained by loading gauge restrictions, and the necessity to make the required ancillary equipment as compact as possible.

Most combined crane locomotives had conventional horizontal locomotive type boilers, with control of both locomotive and crane from the footplate. However, there were also vertical-boilered machines, some of these mounted on separate carriages with their own cylinders and motion, thus resembling self-propelled locomotive cranes, but as they meet our definition have therefore been included in this book for completeness.

The first recorded example of a crane locomotive was a rebuild of an existing engine carried out by the London & North Western Railway in 1866, while two years later Glasgow engineers Dübs & Company designed and built a new locomotive for use in their own works. Over the ensuing eighty or so years nearly 250 were constructed in the United Kingdom, with the last built in 1950 by Robert Stephenson & Hawthorn for an overseas customer.

The combined crane locomotive – very often referred to as a crane tank – appears to have largely been a British concept, although many were built as export orders, but a small number are known to have been built by continental European makers – including two firms that produced fireless examples. The major Australian railway concerns embraced the idea, using both British purpose-built and converted examples, plus locally constructed machines.

Virtually all the machines described in this book are based around a steam locomotive, with lifting functions using either steam or hydraulic power, with the exception of a few electric crane locomotives built in the Edwardian era. Diesel shunting locomotives have also been fitted with cranes for yard and permanent way work into more modern times, but are beyond the scope of this work.

The book is divided into two parts: Part One deals with crane locomotives built and converted by mainline railway companies, while Part Two explains the story of those built by private locomotive building firms.

PART ONE

Crane Locomotives of British Main Line Railways

The first known example of a crane locomotive was a rebuild carried out by the London & North Western Railway in 1866, and over the years various other main line railway companies followed suit, converting existing locomotives for use as cranes. Perhaps surprisingly, only three main line railway companies in Britain constructed new crane locomotives, although at least one other prepared designs.

The engine selected by the LNWR was from a class of 2-4-0 tender locomotives, known as *Crewe Goods* and designed by Francis Trevithick, son of the pioneer Richard Trevithick, who had become Locomotive Superintendent of the then new Crewe works in 1843.

LNWR No. 3074 was similar to the three early conversions, seen here *c.* 1890.

No. 273 *Hope* had been built in September 1851, but fifteen years later was rebuilt with a new boiler and side tanks created by reusing platework from its old tender.

Two further members of the class, Nos 131 *Kingfisher* and 303 *Booth* were similarly rebuilt in 1873. *Booth* had in fact been sold by the LNWR to the Lancaster & Carlisle Railway in 1857, but returned to its original owner just two years later with its takeover of the L&CR, subsequently being renumbered 519. All three served in their new roles until 1892/3, to be replaced by purpose-built machines.

In 1863, John Ramsbottom of the London & North Western Railway introduced a class of small four-coupled saddle tanks for shunting work, and their 4-foot-diameter driving wheels were the first to have the LNWR's distinctive H-section cast-iron, spoked style. Another curious aspect of the design was the use of circular marine-style fireboxes. Twenty-nine years later Francis Webb dusted off the drawings and adapted the design to a lengthened 0-4-2 format with a pair of 3-foot 9-inch-diameter trailing wheels. The extended 'bunker' space was able to accommodate a crane, capable of handling 4-ton loads. The lifting speed for light loads was stated to be 50 feet per minute for light loads, reducing to 14 feet per minute towards the maximum limit. Rail grips were fitted between the coupled axles to increase stability during lifting operations.

Eight such locomotives were built at Crewe works between December 1892 and May 1895, originally with wooden brake blocks and a simple weatherboard, although half-type cabs were later fitted, along with iron brake blocks. Several of the later engines featured a crane with a longer jib, but rated at a maximum 3-ton load. The crane jib could be secured when not in use with chains to the cab structure.

The LNWR 0-4-2 crane tanks were based on the '4-foot goods' introduced by Ramsbottom in 1863, as exemplified by No. 2526.

No. 3248 was turned out by Crewe works in January 1893. Note the chains securing the crane hook to the saddle tank. (Rob Higgins collection)

Ex-works at Crewe in LMS days. No. 3249 was one of the batch of eight cranes built by the London & North Western Railway between 1892 and 1894. (Paul Sankey)

Sister locomotive No. 3248 stands between duties at Crewe on 1 August 1938. (Paul Sankey)

The original Crewe numbers allocated at building were altered within a year or two of construction, and the engines received the running numbers 3246–3252. Two locomotives (3437/8) were transferred from Crewe works to Wolverton carriage works in February and August 1895, where they received departmental numbers 2 and 4. In a confusing series of transfers, No. 4 was transferred back to capital stock only six months later as No. 1842, becoming No. 3310 a year later, before being sent back to Wolverton as its No. 5. The other cranes remained in service with the locomotive department, with the final withdrawals in 1947.

The first two new builds, however, were six-coupled tank locomotives designed by T. W. Worsdell, denoted Class H1, for the North Eastern Railway for lifting and shunting at Gateshead works. Essentially the design was an adaptation of the company's 0-4-0T Class H (later Y7), with extended frames and a third trailing coupled axle. The 3-ton steam crane was fitted in the bunker, but the major components were identical to the H/Y7 class. Following the grouping, the crane tanks were reclassified J78 by the London & North Eastern Railway.

Two locomotives were built in 1888 and given the numbers 590 and 995. As built, they did not have cabs, merely a basic weatherboard, but a simple half-cab was added at a later date. There were minor differences between the two – 590 had 13-inch-diameter cylinders while those of 995 were slightly larger at 14 inches, although both had a stroke length of 20 inches. The jib of 590 was lengthened from 10 feet 6 inches to 12 feet, which resulted in a corresponding slight reduction of safe working load.

In their early days the side tanks of both engines bore the legend 'Gateshead Works', but later this was replaced by the more usual 'NER' initials. No. 995 did indeed spend most of its career at Gateshead, but No. 590 had found its way to Hartlepool by 1907, and by the early 1920s it served for a time at Darlington, Springhead and Percy Main. Both were loaned to Immingham Docks for Admiralty service for several months in 1918.

Having spent their NER careers as service stock, following the grouping the London & North Eastern Railway transferred them to running stock in August 1926, and No. 590 found itself as shed pilot at York. The cranes were rarely used, if at all, in their later years. No. 995 was sold to Hartley Main Colliery in 1933, where it was renumbered 26 and continued to work until withdrawn and scrapped in 1943. Sister No. 590 remained with the LNER, but was withdrawn and scrapped in 1937.

William Adams was Locomotive Superintendent of the North London Railway from 1855 until 1873, and shortly before his departure for pastures new at the Great Eastern Railway arranged the conversion of an 0-4-0 saddle tank, which had been delivered the North & South West Junction Railway in 1858 for use on the South Acton to Hammersmith line. A product of Sharp, Stewart & Company of Manchester in 1872, the inside cylinder locomotive was fitted with a lengthened frame, a pair of trailing wheels and a 3-ton steam crane for use at Bow works. The crane was situated at the rear of the footplate and, as originally converted, the locomotive had no cab and prominent

NER No. 995 has been sent from Gateshead to assist the breakdown gangs following the accident at Felling on 26 March 1907. (W. Embleton)

LNER branding has not yet been applied to former North Eastern Railway No. 590, seen here in the Gateshead shed. (Paul Sankey)

No. 995 is seen here again following its sale to Hartley Main colliery. (W. Embleton)

Salter safety valves. During a subsequent rebuild it was fitted with a cab, Ramsbottom type safety valves, and new 3-foot 10-inch-diameter H section spoked driving wheels. The trailing wheels had a diameter of 2 feet 7 inches, cylinders were 13-inch diameter and 17-inch stroke, with a boiler pressure of 120 pounds per square inch. When taken over by the North London in 1860 it was numbered 37, only to be renumbered 29 one year later, but immediately after conversion carried no number, bearing the lettering 'Steam Crane' on the bunker sides. It underwent further renumbering, first to 29A with the NLR, No. 2896 of the London & North Western Railway in 1922, becoming LMS No. 7217 in 1925 and No. 27217 ten years later. It survived into the British Railways era as its No. 58865 and was finally withdrawn at the age of ninety-three in 1951, having spent most of its life at Bow.

Adams moved to the London & South Western Railway in 1878, where his designs included the B4 class 0-4-0T for yard and dock shunting. A total of twenty of these little outside-cylindered side tanks were built at Nine Elms between 1891 and 1893, but in 1894 Adams produced a crane tank variant, with lengthened frame and pair of trailing wheels. In November of that year an order was placed for three engines, to cost £1,485 each, for use at Nine Elms Works, Northam (at that time a major locomotive depot) and Wimbledon. However, it was subsequently decided that the intended work could be done more cost effectively by self-propelled yard cranes, and the order was cancelled.

The South Devon Railway was the broad-gauge line between Exeter and Plymouth/Torquay, which had been engineered by Brunel. It became part of the Great Western Railway

The former North London Railway crane tank, as LMS No. 27217, at Devons Road shed *c.* 1938. (Paul Sankey)

No. 27217 spent much of its life at Bow works, where it is seen in August 1937. (Paul Sankey)

In 1894, William Adams produced a crane locomotive design for the London & South Western Railway based on the B4 class dock shunter, although an order for three of them was subsequently cancelled.

in February 1876, at a time when three 2-4-0 saddle tank locomotives were in build at the company's Newton Abbot works, with major components supplied by the Wigan-based Ince Forge Company. The partially constructed engines were taken to Swindon, where they were completed as standard-gauge side tanks, emerging as numbers 1298/9/1300 in December 1878. With 4-foot 0-inch-diameter coupled wheels and 3-foot 0-inch leading wheels they weighed only 22 tons and 12 cwt in full working order. In April 1881, No. 1299 was rebuilt with an extended 14-foot wheelbase, slightly larger cylinders of 12-inch, diameter bore and 17-inch stroke, and fitted with a 1½-ton crane, which increased its weight to 28 tons 12 cwt. For the next twelve years it was employed by the Engineers' Department at Reading, but by the 1920s it was working at Swindon works and was reboilered in 1925. It outlived its non-converted sisters, which had been allocated to Exeter to work the Culm Valley Light Railway, to be withdrawn in September 1936 and finally scrapped some eighteen months later. As designed by South Devon the three locomotives were allocated the names *Saturn*, *Jupiter* and *Mercury*, which they never actually carried.

All the mainline company cranes described so far were essentially conventional tank locomotives designed or adapted to accommodate a crane at the rear end, sometimes with one additional axle, but three crane locomotives built by the Great Western Railway adopted a more novel approach, using a six-coupled pannier tank, with a frame extended at the rear to accommodate a four-wheel trailing bogie. The crane mounting was located directly over the bogie pin.

Great Western Railway No. 1299 was one of a trio built in 1878 from parts ordered by the South Devon Railway. However, No. 1299 was rebuilt with a crane in 1881, and remained at work until 1936. (John Law)

Shortly before his retirement as Chief Locomotive Engineer, William Dean ordered the construction of two such locomotives from Swindon works in 1901. With works numbers 1774/5 they were named *Cyclops* and *Steropes* with running numbers 17 and 18 respectively. A third locomotive, No. 16 *Hercules,* followed twenty years later in 1921, during the Churchward era. The engines were based on the 850 class of saddle tanks that had been introduced as early as 1874, but fitted with pannier tanks, which would become such a classic Great Western feature. The boilers were domeless, which, with the flat-topped tanks, allowed a supporting crutch for the crane jibs to be fitted.

The crane capacity was 6 tons at a radius of 18 feet using double chains, but with treble chains this could be increased to 9 tons at 12-foot radius. The substantial nature of the design resulted in a total weight in working order of 63 tons.

The three locomotives worked at Swindon and Stafford Road Wolverhampton until withdrawn in September 1936, being scrapped the following year.

In 1861, Beyer Peacock introduced a standard design 2-4-0T for lighter passenger and branch line duties, which continued to be built for some twenty years. Early customers included the West Midland and Isle of Wight Railways. Three such locomotives were built in 1873 for the East & West Junction Railway, which operated between Stratford upon Avon and Towcester, and a company that found itself in such financial difficulty that the new locomotives were returned to the builders. They were eventually sold in May 1875 to the Lancashire & Yorkshire Railway, which allocated the numbers 517/8/9. In 1891, No. 518 was taken into Horwich works and fitted with a 3-ton steam crane in the bunker. As a counterweight the original timber front buffer beam was replaced with a heavier unit consisting of two 1½-inch-thick steel plates with a 5½-inch-thick lead sandwich filling.

Cyclops was one of a pair of locomotives ordered by the GWR in 1901, based on a standard pannier tank design with extended rear frame and bogie to accommodate a crane for use at Swindon and Wolverhampton works. (John Law)

Another view of *Cyclops* in Swindon yard. A third crane, named *Hercules*, was built in 1921, but all were withdrawn in 1936. (Rob Higgins collection)

Beyer Peacock works No. 1239 of 1873, as rebuilt with a crane by the Lancashire & Yorkshire Railway in 1891. (Lancashire & Yorkshire Railway Society collection)

An ex-works view of the Horwich works Beyer Peacock. (Lancashire & Yorkshire Railway Society collection)

The first locomotive with an 0-6-2 wheel arrangement appeared in Britain when William Barton Wright rebuilt an existing Jenkins six-coupled engine with a new trailing radial axle and side tanks in 1877. A batch of ten with many common components was ordered from Messrs Kitson in 1881. These locomotives had 4-foot 6-inch-diameter driving wheels and 17½ x 26-inch cylinders, with a boiler pressure of 140 pounds per square inch, and were given the numbers 141–150 by the L&YR. In 1924, following the withdrawal of Beyer Peacock No. 518, the steam crane was fitted to one of the Kitson tanks – No. 146. Renumbered 11601 by the LMS, it served in this form until withdrawn in 1931.

During his tenure as Locomotive Superintendent of the Great Eastern Railway, Samuel Waite Johnson ordered five six-coupled shunting locomotives from the Lincoln firm of Ruston & Proctor, which were delivered between May and November 1868, and numbered 204–208. They were built without weather protection for the crew, but Johnson's successor, William Adams, who was earlier responsible for the North London crane tank conversion, fitted basic half-type cabs. The first withdrawal, No. 207, came in 1889, but two years later James Holden, who was by then in charge of the locomotive department, took No. 205 into works for conversion as a crane tank. The crane, with a jib 11 feet in length, which could lift 3 tons, was fitted in the bunker, but to accommodate the installation the locomotive's frames and wheelbase were extended. A new boiler was fitted with both a larger diameter barrel and longer firebox – a design that was also being fitted to other locomotive types, including the Bromley E10 0-4-4 tanks.

The rebuilt engine was promptly put to good use at Stratford works and the following year two more – Nos 206 and 208 – were similarly treated, while the final

Barton Wright 0-6-2 No. 146 of the Lancashire & Yorkshire Railway was fitted with the Beyer Peacock's crane in 1924. (Lancashire & Yorkshire Railway Society collection)

One of three works cranes, originally designed by S. W. Johnson, identified simply as *B*, at Stratford in 1932. (Paul Sankey)

J92 class, Crane *C*, at Stratford in 1933. (Paul Sankey)

In July 1948, No. 68867 had been adorned with additional digit of its British Railways number, although still with LNER lettering. (Paul Sankey)

member of the class, No. 205 was withdrawn and scrapped. These three crane tanks, with 4-foot 0-inch-diameter driving wheels, and 16 x 22-inch cylinders lost their numbers at Stratford and were identified as *Works B/C/D*. They were used to assist stripping down locomotives in the works and for transporting components around the site, but by the 1930s the installation of overhead gantry cranes had reduced their workload. Following the grouping in 1923 the LNER classified them as Z4, but redesignated them J92 only four years later. They continued to be identified as *B*, *C* and *D* until 1946 when they became Nos 8667–9. A further renumbering, as Nos 68667–9, followed nationalisation two years later, but in 1950 No. 68669 was withdrawn, followed two years later by sister No. 68667. Despite renumbering as *Departmental No 35* in September 1952, the last survivor was also withdrawn by the end of the year.

The Great Central Railway introduced a class of twelve six-coupled saddle tank shunting locomotives designed by Harry Pollitt and built at Gorton Works in 1897. Intriguingly, they were delivered during the period of the name change from Manchester, Sheffield & Lincoln Railway to the Great Central, and were initially lettered for the outgoing title. They were designed for use in areas with severe curves such as docks and colliery sidings, with allocations at Grimsby, Immingham and Birkenhead. For their dockside duties they were fitted with a warning bell and a hooter rather than the usual whistle. In 1903, John Robinson, the Chief Mechanical Engineer, arranged for No. 889 to be converted into an 0-6-2T with a pair of 2-foot-diameter trailing wheels and sent to the Vulcan Foundry at

Great Central Railway No. 889 as built in June 1897, before conversion with a crane.

No. 889 is shown here as converted by Vulcan Foundry in 1903, and with a trailing axle.

Newton-le-Willows for the fitting of a crane capable of lifting 3½ tons at a 14-feet radius, which, like the other conversions thus far described, was located in the bunker. The rebuilt locomotive was employed as a works shunter at Gorton until it suffered accidental damage in January 1918. It was then returned to its original format, without crane and trailing wheels. The first withdrawals of the class took place in 1935, with the last survivor condemned in 1951.

Patrick Stirling introduced a series of 0-4-4 tank locomotives to the Great Northern Railway, including a batch of six that were fitted with condensing equipment for working London suburban services underground to Moorgate and South London. Number 533 had been built in 1876 and worked as a conventional locomotive until June 1905 when it was fitted with a crane, and in March 1906 it was released for use lifting and shunting at Doncaster works. The crane was capable of taking a 5-ton load at an 11-foot 0-inch jib radius. The conversion also involved a redesign of the water storage arrangements, as the original tank beneath the bunker was displaced by the crane, and two new side tanks were fitted astride the smokebox, which would also have acted as a counterbalance. The new tank sides were lettered 'Doncaster Works'. An Ivatt pattern cab was fitted along with steam sanding equipment, and the vacuum brake was retained. Designed for passenger work, the locomotive had rather large driving wheels for a works shunter, at 5-feet 7-inches in diameter, with 17½-inch diameter and 24-inch-stroke cylinders.

The locomotive had been reboilered in 1891 with a larger, yet still domeless, G2 class unit, and at some later stage it received an Ivatt pattern boiler, with dome, designed for the larger C12 Atlantic-type tanks, which would have been some 15 inches longer than the original. In this form it worked until around 1923 when a major component of the crane failed and it was laid aside, although not formally withdrawn until November 1928.

Great Northern Railway No. 533 of 1876 was converted for use as the Doncaster works crane and shunter in 1906 – a rebuild that included repositioning of the side tanks.

A classmate of former No. 533 was Great Northern Railway No. 513, Doncaster works No. 140 of 1874, which demonstrates its original condition.

Australian Railways

The mainline state railways in Australia used a variety of crane locomotives, both in workshop environments and as coaling cranes. Like their British counterparts they sometimes rebuilt existing locomotives, but they also ordered purpose-built machines from private builders. New South Wales Government Railways became the largest operator, with no fewer than twenty-five examples owned over the years.

In 1890, the New South Wales Government Railways withdrew its entire class of N67 0-6-0 side tank locomotives from Sydney suburban services, as it was considered that their 4-foot-diameter driving wheels were no longer adequate for the speed required, and relegated them to shunting and other duties. The design closely resembled the British Stroudley Terrier class, but were built locally in 1875 by Vale & Lucy or Thomas Mort & Company. In 1900, five locomotives had their bunkers removed to allow the fitting of a crane, with grab for coaling duties, and in their new role were renumbered Lo 14–18, but became 1025–9 in a renumbering scheme of 1924. No. 1029 was withdrawn and scrapped in 1929, but the last examples survived until 1937. The cranes from three of them were, however, retained and fitted to other locomotives. The recipients were 0-6-0 tank

No. 73XX was built by Vale & Lucy in 1875 for New South Wales Government Railways, seen here at Hamilton engine shed shortly after conversion as a coaling crane in 1900. Later renumbered 1027, it was withdrawn in 1937. (University of Newcastle, Ralph Snowball collection)

Upon withdrawal, the cranes from No. 73 and two other condemned locomotives were transferred to three members of the R285 class, which had been built by Vulcan Foundry in 1884.

locomotives from a class of six that had been built in Britain by the Vulcan Foundry in 1885. These engines, which had originally been ordered with a 2- 4- 0T wheel arrangement, were redesignated Z-18 class in 1924.

In late 1937 the bunkers of Nos 1801/3/4 were removed and replaced by the cranes. Renumbered yet again as 1076–8, they were added to the X10 class – a mixed bag of miscellaneous shunters and cranes – but post-Second World War they reverted to normal locomotives. Two have survived: Nos 1076 (formerly 1804) and 1077 (formerly 1803).

No. 1076 was overhauled and fitted with a Beyer Peacock boiler in 1966 and continued in use as a shunter and a stationary boiler until 1971. Set aside for preservation, it was stored outside for many years, but in 2008 it was taken to the Goulbourn Roundhouse, where it had worked in the 1950s, for restoration and was returned to steam in 2017. Its sister has been cosmetically restored in a blue livery as *Thomas the Tank Engine*.

Three further locomotives from the F351 class of 2-4-0 tanks were similarly converted. These had been built for Sydney suburban passenger work by Beyer Peacock in Manchester and locally by Henry Vale, but were relegated to shunting duties in 1902 following a serious derailment. Originally numbered F358/9/65, they became Nos 1035/6/42 when transferred to the X10 class. Two lost their cranes in 1914, while No. 1042 retained one until 1937 and still survives.

Victoria Railways bought a six-coupled crane tank from the Scottish builder Dübs in 1891, which it named *Crane No 2*, and two years later constructed a locomotive, without crane, but otherwise almost identical in dimensions and appearance to the Dübs product. Numbered Z 256, this was actually the first locomotive to be built at the company's Newport, Melbourne, works, and was intended for suburban services. However, in 1903, it too was fitted with a crane, for use at the north Melbourne works – officially *No 3 Crane*, but generally known as *Polly*. It spent the last few years of its career at the South Dynon Diesel Workshops and was not withdrawn until as late as 16 June 1978. In 1983, it was cosmetically restored by apprentices to its original condition – without the crane.

Subsequently, four more identical locomotives with cranes were built at Newport between 1910 and 1924, and numbered as cranes 4/8/9/15, all of which remained in service until scrapped in the 1960s. The Victoria cranes usually worked either coupled to a shunter's wagon, which was equipped with wide steps and grab rails and also provided space for an additional coal supply, or with an old locomotive tender to extend operating range and permit the occasional foray onto the mainline if required.

In 1856 and 1858, Robert Stephenson had built two 2-4-0 tender locomotives, works Nos 1047 and 1084 respectively, for service on the South Australian Railways 5-foot 6-inch broad-gauge system. Designated Class B, the SAR numbered them B4 and B7. Between November 1875 and February 1876, they were both rebuilt as 2-4-0 well tanks and their tenders discarded. In May 1887, No. B7 was fitted with a crane and side tanks, while its sister was similarly converted in 1893. No. B7 was condemned in 1935 while No. B4 soldiered on for another three years until it too was withdrawn in 1938.

Tasmanian Railways bought fifteen 4-4-0 tender locomotives, which formed its Class B, from Beyer Peacock in Manchester between 1884 and 1892. Five were withdrawn in 1936, but one was fitted with a crane, the jib fitted to the locomotive frames in front of the smokebox, with the hoisting gear mounted on the tender – a most unusual arrangement, which did not permit any slewing function. As such, it was used in the Hobart yards.

Crane No 2, the original Dübs-built example, is seen in later life at North Melbourne in November 1961. (Weston Langford)

Crane No 3 was still at work at North Melbourne yard, coupled with an old tender, in January 1967. (Weston Langford)

Although it looks identical to a Dübs product, *Crane No 3* was actually the first locomotive built at the Newport workshops of Victoria Railways in 1893, although not converted to a crane until 1903. It is seen here with tender at North Melbourne locomotive depot in January 1965. (Weston Langford)

After withdrawal in 1978, *Crane No 3*, was restored to original condition as No. Z526 *Polly*.

Crane No 8 was one of a further four locomotives built at Melbourne, completed in 1916 and scrapped in 1965. It is seen coupled with a shunter's wagon at Ballarat North, 20 August 1964. (Weston Langford)

Originally built in 1858 by Robert Stephenson as a tender locomotive for South Australia Railways, No. B4 was twice rebuilt: first as a well tank in 1875 and then again in 1893 with a 2-ton crane. As such, it survived until 1938. (Chris Drymalik)

Crane tank No. B4 after its first rebuild as a 2-4-0 well tank. (Chris Drymalik)

No. B7 was similarly rebuilt, another Robert Stephenson product, works No. 1084 of 1858, seen here at Kingsborough. (Chris Drymalik)

PART TWO

Crane Locomotives by Private Builders

A variety of private locomotive building firms in Britain constructed crane locomotives both for the domestic market and for export. In terms of numbers built, Hawthorn Leslie and its successor Robert Stephenson & Hawthorns was dominant, with a tally of over eighty – more than twice as many as the next two firms, Dübs and Andrew Barclay, which each produced just under forty. Other firms that constructed many thousands of steam locomotives were each responsible for just a few built with cranes. While some designs featured a more or less conventional locomotive with a crane mounted at the rear of the footplate, similar to the mainline company machines already described, others featured a crane positioned centrally over the boiler, with a separate supporting structure, with yet a further variant using the boiler itself as part of the crane mounting. The Glasgow-based firm of Neilson even mounted the central crane pillar around the chimney and smokebox. While steam-operated crane mechanisms were most commonly employed, there were examples of hydraulic power too. Virtually all the machines described in this section were more or less conventional locomotives fitted with a crane, either constructed by the builder or bought in from a crane maker. However, a number of vertical-boilered cranes constructed by specialist makers who built large numbers of self-propelled locomotive cranes, fall within our earlier definition of a crane locomotive as having separate cylinders for propulsion, and thus the boundary lines are not always clear.

Dübs & Company

The first crane locomotive by an independent firm was built by in Glasgow by Dübs & Company in 1868 for use at their own Queens Park, Polmadie, works, which had been established four years earlier. This was followed a year later by an order from Edward Corry for a locomotive of 5-foot gauge for Russia. Corry was a merchant dealing in copper and iron but was also involved in railway development schemes not only in Russia, but South America, Spain, India and Ireland. As London agent for

Dübs & Company, he also ordered another slightly smaller locomotive two years later on behalf of H. B. Froom & Company. The cranes of these locomotives were mounted directly on the boiler barrel, the first two (works Nos 237 and 302) fitted with cylinders of 12-inch diameter and 22-inch stroke, with 3-foot 6-inch-diameter driving wheels, while the third (works No. 435 of 1871) had 9-inch-diameter cylinders and 2-foot 6-inch-diameter wheels.

The cranes on later locomotives were mounted on a separate structure, fixed to the main frames and straddling the boiler, and this became the company's standard method of construction. Over the following decade a series of orders followed for a total of seven locomotives for the Steel Company of Scotland, the first three with 10-inch-diameter x 20-inch-stroke cylinders and 3-foot-diameter driving wheels, and subsequently larger 12 x 22-inch cylinders with wheels of 3 feet 6 inches or 3 feet 7 inches in diameter. The bigger engines weighed a total of 34 tons, while the smaller locomotives were somewhat lighter at only 24 tons. This particular customer had operated several sites in the Glasgow area, at Hallside, Clydebridge and the Blochairn Ironworks, which was acquired in 1880. The Blochairn takeover and expansion at Hallside resulted in orders for four new locomotives in 1880–81: works Nos 1373/4 and 1506/7. In the years 1877–79 three other crane tanks were built for Panteg steelworks in South Wales, the New Russia Company and New South Wales Government Railways – the first of several orders for Australia.

DUBS & C?. GLASGOW LOCOMOTIVE WORKS.

The first Dübs crane, No. 237, was built for the company's own use in 1868.

The second Dübs crane, built in the following year, was destined for Russia.

A sectioned view of an early 1869 Dübs crane, which illustrates the initial method of mounting the crane directly on the boiler.

The crane mounting structure can be clearly seen in this view of Dübs No. 2250 of 1886 pictured with tanks removed during restoration at Thirlmere, New South Wales. (Ed Slee)

The Consett Iron Company placed its first order for a crane locomotive with Dübs in 1883, works No. 1758, which it numbered D No 1. A second engine, works No. 2063, followed a year later as Consett's D No. 2, with two more – Dübs 2365/6, Consett D Nos 4/5 – in 1888. The Consett company eventually operated the largest fleet of crane locomotives in Britain.

Crane locomotives were proving themselves particularly useful in the iron and steel industry, with orders from Weardale Iron Company and the Brymbo Steel Company in 1884, plus the Glasgow-based British Hydraulic Foundry in 1892.

In 1891, works No. 2711 was completed for the Victoria Government Railways in Australia, which was the only six-coupled crane locomotive built by Dübs. Built for 5-foot 3-inch gauge, it had 3-foot 6-inch-diameter wheels, 14 x 22-inch cylinders and a crane with a 5-ton capacity lift. In working order it weighed 35 tons 10 cwt. After a working life spent mainly at Newport Works, it was withdrawn in February 1970, but has been preserved at the Railway Museum, North Williamstown, Melbourne. A standard four-coupled crane tank built by Dübs in 1886, works No. 2250, for the New South Wales Government Railways has been preserved at the Trainworks Museum, Thirlmere.

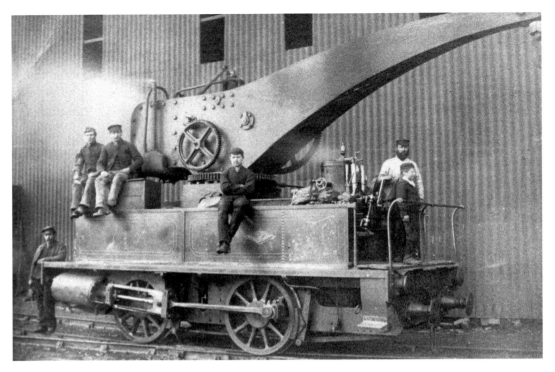

Dübs works No. 2051 of 1884 is seen here at the Tudhoe works of the Weardale Iron Company, *c.* 1890. (TSLHS Harry Spence collection)

New South Wales Government Railways' No. 1030, Dübs works No. 1237 of 1879, is seen at Clyde Depot during the 1940s.

Works No. 2711 of 1890, the only six-coupled crane built by Dübs, for Australia's Victoria Railways, as its *Crane No. 2*. (Chris Drymalik)

Another product of 1891 was No. 2758 for the Buenos Aires Great Southern Railway, and this was followed by No. 2840 for the New Russia Company. Both of these were fitted with 10 x 20-inch cylinders and 3-foot-diameter wheels. The company built another locomotive for its own yard use in 1893, No. 3080, and between 1896 and 1898, three more followed for the New Russia Company. In 1899, No. 3693 was supplied to the Calcutta Corporation Municipal Railway, which ran an extensive system as part as part of the city's waste disposal operation, while in 1901 No. 4101 was built to the order of Shelton Iron & Steel Company at Stoke on Trent. This latter engine worked until 1968 when it was acquired for preservation – initially at Cranmore with the East Somerset Railway, but later returned to Staffordshire, joining the industrial locomotive collection at the Foxfield Railway. During its working life it was reboilered by Kerr Stuart in 1921 and converted to oil firing in 1961, but has since reverted to coal. Two further locomotives were built for the Steel Company of Scotland, No. 3694 of 1899 and No. 4239 of 1902, allocated the fleet Nos 4 and 5 respectively.

In 1903, Dübs was one of the three constituent companies, along with Sharp Stewart and Neilson, which amalgamated to form the North British Locomotive Company, at

Crane No. 1034, Dübs 2250, shunting at Eveleigh Works, New South Wales in 1964. (Graeme Skeet)

which time Dübs employed roughly 2,000 people, was building around 160 locomotives each year and had turned out thirty-five crane locomotives since 1868. The Dübs crane tank was adopted as a standard design by the new company. It was available in five sizes with crane capacities ranging from 2½ to 6 tons and jib radii from 12 to 16 feet, but only four were subsequently built by North British. Two were completed at Dübs' own former Queens Park works in 1906/7, one each for the Steel Company of Scotland and New South Wales Government Railways, but they were allocated works numbers in a new series of Nos 17263 and 18086 respectively. The Australian engine was allocated running number Lo 04, but amended in 1924 to No. 1044, the identity it retained until scrapped

The recently formed North British Locomotive Company built this crane for Argentina in 1907, which is now stored at the Ferroclub Haedo Museum. (Matias Chiodini)

The North British Company, in essence, continued with the Dübs crane locomotive design, with three size specifications offered in 1910. (Alon Siton)

in 1969. The third went to the Buenos Aries Western Railway, Argentina, as its number 71V in 1907, where it survives in preservation, as does Dübs No. 2758 of 1891. The fourth locomotive, No. 21522 of 1917, was constructed at Hyde Park works, previously Neilson's premises, for Consett Iron Company as its D No. 14.

Once the separate framework for the crane structure became standard practice, the basic design varied little over the years. The crane slewing engine was mounted over the right-hand side of the boiler/side tank, with the hoisting mechanism, which could be specified with various gearing ratios, mounted in the jib structure. Other minor locomotive variations included single slide bars and Laird crossheads.

In more recent times the Dübs design became the prototype for Harvey the Crane Engine in the *Thomas the Tank Engine* stories.

Neilson & Company

Before he sent up his own company, Henry (or Heinrich) Dübs, who had been born in 1816 in Germany, had been works manager and partner at Neilson & Company, another Glasgow concern that could trace its origins back to 1836 when founded by Walter Neilson and James Mitchell. In 1861, three years before Dübs left, taking a number of staff with him, the company opened its new Hyde Park Works at Springburn.

The company built a total of six crane tanks over a twenty-year period, all to a similar basic design, which most notably featured the crane at the front of the locomotive with the central pillar of the crane surrounding the chimney with supporting operating mechanism to the smokebox sides.

The first of the four-wheeled, four-coupled engines was turned out in 1875, with works No. 2012 for the company's own works use as its Yard No. 1.

Three years later works No. 2408 followed to the order of the Caledonian Railway, which numbered it 485 and used until withdrawn and scrapped in 1908. There then followed two locomotives for the South Eastern Railway, works No. 2686 in 1881 and No. 4891 in 1895. The SER numbered them 302 and 409, with No. 302 just surviving into the British Railways era, being withdrawn in 1949, while its sister succumbed during Southern Railway days in 1935. In between the orders for the two SER engines, works No. 4004 was supplied to Hodbarrow Mining Company for use at its Millom haematite mine in Cumbria. Known as *Snipey*, and numbered 6 in the mine company's fleet, it was still working into the late 1960s and has fortunately been preserved at a private museum in Lytham St Annes. The last of the sextet was No. 5071, built in 1896 for James Millar & Company as No. 1 at its nearby Stobcross works.

All six locomotives had 11-inch-diameter x 20-inch-stroke cylinders, but there were variations in wheelbase and driving wheel diameter. Nos 2408, 2686 and 4891 had a wheelbase of 5 feet 9 inches with 3-foot 3-inch-diameter wheels, while No. 5071 had a longer wheelbase at 6 feet 6 inches. Water tank capacity was only 200 gallons, and bunker capacity was 5cwt. The boiler, with a grate area of 7 square feet, was pressed to 120 pounds per square inch.

The positioning of the crane required an extended overhang at the footplate end of the locomotive to act as a counterbalance and resulted in a leading axle loading of 6 tons 11

The Southern Railway inherited two Neilson crane tanks, which had originally been built for the South Eastern Railway. S234, works No. 2686, was originally used at Folkestone Harbour, and later at Ashford and Lancing works, until withdrawn in 1949. (Paul Sankey)

A Neilson works view of No. 4004 before delivery to Hodbarrow.

Neilson works No. 4004 was supplied to Hodbarrow Mining Company, where it was still at work as late as 1967. (Leslie Pitcher)

The hoisting engine at the rear of the jib and the slewing engine on the side of *Snipey's* smokebox are clearly demonstrated in this view. (Leslie Pitcher)

cwt, but 11 tons 6 cwt at the rear. The slewing engine for the crane was mounted vertically at the side of the smokebox, while the hoisting mechanism was located at the rear of the crane structure itself.

One of the South Eastern engines, No. 2686, could lift 2½ tons with a jib of 7-foot 2-inch radius, while its sister, and the Caledonian engine, had jib lengths of 8 feet 6 inches, which permitted a load of 2 tons. The last one built, No. 5071, had an even longer 10-foot-radius jib, which reduced the maximum lift to only 1½ tons.

The company became Neilson Reid & Company in 1898, and five years later amalgamated with Dübs and Sharp Stewart to become the North British Locomotive Company.

The Kilmarnock Builders

Glasgow was not the only centre of crane locomotive building in Scotland, as over forty examples were produced by three firms based in Kilmarnock. The great majority of these emerged from Caledonia Works of Andrew Barclay Sons & Company over a period from 1881 to 1947. Andrew Barclay's first business ventures as a young man, in 1829, related to producing millshafts, gas lamps, and then colliery winding engines. These ultimately ended in failure, but in 1859 he set up a new locomotive building firm, specialising in four-coupled tank locomotives for industrial use.

However, in 1871, Andrew Barclay helped set up another locomotive building concern with his brother John and four sons. The new firm was also based in Kilmarnock, at the River Bank Works, and perhaps confusingly was known as Barclays & Company. The new venture was apparently declared bankrupt in the mid-1870s, but it survived until the business was merged into Andrew Barclay Sons & Company in 1888. During its separate existence, the company built one crane locomotive in 1881, works No. 286, followed by a second four years later – both four-coupled side tanks that were supplied to the Motherwell works of David Colville & Sons as its fleet Nos 4 and 6. No. 4 was rebuilt in 1942 and later passed to Dixon's Ironworks at Govan, being scrapped in September 1960 after the closure of the works, while No. 6 was sold to Motherwell Machinery & Scrap in 1928.

Coincidentally, Andrew Barclay also built its first crane locomotive in the same year, another four-coupled side tank, which proved to be of a very similar design to the Barclay product. With cylinder dimensions of 12-inch diameter and 18-inch stroke, works No. 223 was supplied to John Orr Ewing & Company of Alexandria, Dumbarton, a company engaged in the textile and dyeing industry. There followed an interval of eight years before the next one, No. 646 was built for the locomotive-building company Sharp, Stewart, which also took delivery of a second example in 1902. The next crane locomotive built in 1895 went to Germany for the Grand Duchy of Baden State Railway as its No. 149, while the Glasgow Corporation Sewage Department ordered a slightly smaller engine with 9-inch-diameter cylinders and 3-foot-diameter wheels for delivery the following year as its No. 1. The other crane completed in 1896, works No. 777, was the first of many for Stanton Ironworks at Ilkeston Derbyshire, with another, works No. 855 following three years later as *Stanton No 10*. In the interim period, three more, of varying dimensions, were built for David Colville, Steel Company of Scotland and the Smelting Corporation.

All the crane locomotives to date were of the same basic pattern – 0-4-0 wheel arrangement with side tanks – but of varying dimensions, crane design and capacity. The entire Andrew Barclay output featured a crane mounted on a framework straddling the boiler and fixed to the main frames, but the positioning of the operating mechanism varied. The earliest engines were built with a slewing engine each side of the boiler, with the hoisting engine, an inverted twin-cylinder vee arrangement on top of the firebox. This was superseded by a layout that utilised an inverted two-cylinder vee engine each side of the crane frame, which required a cut-out in each of the side tanks. A third arrangement used a vertical slewing engine each side of the firebox, and hoisting engine between dome and crane, i.e. forward of the crane structure.

Several types of jib could be specified: a fixed structure with a hoisting function and built in counterweight constructed of steel plate, or one capable of derricking or luffing, by which means the jib height and radius could be altered. The latter option was normally a girder-based construction with tie rods and separate counterweight.

In 1900, works No. 878 was built for a Swedish customer, Vagn Ock Maskinfabriks Aktie Bolaget of Falun. This locomotive had a well tank rather than side tanks, plus an enclosed cab, 3-foot-diameter wheels and 11-inch-diameter x 18-inch-stroke cylinders. All Barclay crane tanks were outside cylindered and most used Stephenson motion with inside valves, but No. 878 was the first of several to be specified with Walschaert's valve gear. Fitted with a luffing jib, at some point in its career the crane was removed, and it continued in use until 1958, when, with boiler, cylinders and motion removed it was converted to a diesel locomotive.

In this 1920s view crew and colleagues pose with their locomotive, thought to be Andrew Barclay No. 777 of 1896 or No. 855 of 1899, at Riddings Ironworks. (Tony Fisher)

Shipbuilders Denny Brothers of Dumbarton bought works No. 1058 in 1905, and four years later, in 1909, the largest and heaviest crane locomotive built at Kilmarnock, works No. 1190, was delivered to a Canadian customer, the General Mining Association (Sydney Mines), as its No. 13, named *Harvey Graham*, later passing to the Nova Scotia Steel & Coal Company. This was an impressive eight-coupled machine, with 17-inch-diameter x 22-inch-stroke cylinders, Walschaert's valve gear, wheels of 3-foot 5-inch diameter, with a 12-foot wheelbase and a boiler pressure of 200 pounds per square inch. The machine weighed 65 tons in working order, and the crane could lift 8 tons at 16-foot radius. It had a fully enclosed cab and a rear bunker with a coal capacity of 2 tons. It was scrapped in 1930.

The next three cranes were also export orders, with Nos 1323 and 1346 sent to Australia in 1913, one each for the Commonwealth and New South Wales Government Railways, with the third, No. 1426, destined for the United Steel Corporation of South Africa in 1916. This latter engine was built to a 3-foot 6-inch gauge with outside frames and Walschaert's valve gear.

David Colville ordered two more for the Motherwell steelworks: Nos 1463 and 1504 – the former 14 x 22-inch cylinders and 3-foot 3-inch-diameter wheels, while the other was slightly larger with 15-inch-diameter cylinders and 3-foot 5-inch diameter wheels.

In 1900 Andrew Barclay supplied well tank crane No. 878 to Vagn Ock Maskinfabricks of Falun, Sweden. (Jarnvags Museet)

Christened *Jumbo*, the crane was removed from No. 878 in 1916, but it continued to serve as works shunter for many years. (Jarnvags Museet)

In the 1950s *Jumbo* was rebuilt as a diesel shunter, and was finally retired in 1977. (Jarnvags Museet)

The British Admiralty ordered a six-coupled crane for dockyard use, No. 1507 of 1917, with 10 x 16-inch cylinders and 2-foot 9-inch-diameter wheels, an altogether unusual machine with a luffing jib of steel plate construction, which could lift a maximum of 2½ tons. The crane engines were of the inverted vee-twin type, mounted each side of the crane frame, which resulted in substantial 'cut-outs' to the tank sides. The locomotive also had Walschaert's motion, an enclosed cab and rear coal bunker. Another crane, works No. 2027, was supplied to the Admiralty twenty years later in 1937. Intended for use in Portsmouth Dockyard as its No. 7, this was a more conventional four-coupled locomotive, but with lattice

Andrew Barclay No. 1323 of 1913 was supplied to Commonwealth Railways of Australia as its No. 2 crane and is seen here at Port Augusta works in December 1951. (the late Douglas Colquhoun, Chris Drymalik collection)

girder luffing jib, with a lifting capacity of 1¼ tons at a radius of 20 feet. The Walschaert's motion was partially enclosed by side sheets. In 1952, by which time it had lost its crane, it was transferred to the Admiralty depot at Dalmuir, where it was renumbered DR2 but apparently never used. After ten years in store it was scrapped in September 1963.

The next five cranes built were all standard pattern locomotives with 14-inch diameter x 22-inch-stroke cylinders and 3-foot 5-inch diameter wheels. Works Nos 1580, 1582 and 1615 were all supplied in 1918 to Coltness Iron Company, Newmains, Coventry Ordnance Works and Beardmore & Company, Dalmuir, respectively. Works Nos 1665 and 1715 followed in 1920 for Consett Iron Company as its numbers D No. 16 and D No. 17. The Consett company subsequently ordered one more Barclay crane, works No. 2111 in 1942.

Between 1925 and 1937 no less than seven cranes were built for Stanton Ironworks. This became a fairly well-known operation, with crane locomotives working into the 1960s. Fortunately, one has survived: Stanton No. 24, which worked at the company's Ilkeston site until 1967, when transferred to Riddings. Final withdrawal came in 1969, but the locomotive is now fortunately preserved at the Midland Railway Centre, Butterley. During its career at Ilkeston it gained the nickname *Legfast*, following a runaway incident.

Two further locomotives were turned out during the Second World War. The first was in 1942 for Clyde Alloy Steel at Motherwell and was fitted with an electromagnet for lifting scrap metal. The magnet was powered by a steam turbo generator and Barclays were granted a patent in 1941 for a slip-ring device within the crane structure to retain power supply to the magnet without impeding slewing ability. The magnet was removed in 1953

An unidentified Andrew Barclay crane tank loads pipes at Staveley Wharf, Nutbrook Canal, in 1937. The motorboat *Colonel* was originally steam powered, but had been converted to diesel by the time of this photograph. (the Late Hugh Compton, Richard Thomas collection)

Taking water at Riddings Ironworks, which had been founded by James Oakes & Company but was taken over by Stanton in 1920. (Tony Fisher)

Three unidentified members of the Stanton Ironworks fleet await their next turn in 1955. (John Phillips)

Stanton Ironworks No. 26, Andrew Barclay works No. 1928 of 1927, prepares to shunt a wagon loaded with pipes in January 1967. (Les Pitcher)

when the Craignneuk Works site at Motherwell was closed, and the locomotive, works No. 2127, was transferred to Colville's Glengarnock Steelworks in Ayrshire as its No. 6. British Steel, successors to Colville, donated it to the Scottish Railway Preservation Society in 1978, and it has been restored for display at the Bo'ness & Kinneil Railway. Locomotive No. 2152, which would be the penultimate crane locomotive built at Caledonia Works, was supplied to Dorman Long at Middlesbrough in 1943.

The final order was for Tata Steel in India, works No. 2231, and delivered in 1947. With an 0-6-2 wheel arrangement and 14½-inch-diameter x 20-inch-stroke cylinders with Walschaert's valve gear, the crane had a lifting capacity of 6 tons.

While this was the last crane locomotive built, Andrew Barclay continued to produce conventional and fireless steam locomotives for industrial use well into the following decade, plus diesel locomotives for both private customers and British Railways.

The third builder of crane locomotives in Kilmarnock was Grant, Ritchie & Company, which operated from Townholme Engine Works. The firm had originally been founded as Grant Brothers, and locomotive building represented only one aspect of the business, along with plant for steelworks, colliery winding and pumping engines, plus other general engineering work.

Of the forty-five locomotives built between 1879 and 1920, three were equipped with cranes. Each of these was an 0-4-0 side tank with 12-inch diameter and 22-inch-stroke outside cylinders. The first was works No. 209, delivered in 1890 to the Glengarnock Iron & Steel Company in Ayrshire, which was subsequently taken over by David Colville & Sons

Barclay works No. 2127 of 1942 was supplied with an electromagnet for handling scrap at Clyde Alloy Steels, but stands out of use at Glengarnock steelworks in 1975. (Paul Bryson)

The view from the footplate of now-preserved Andrew Barclay works No. 2127 of 1942, showing the vee-twin hoisting engine. (Alastair Mather)

Glenfield No. 1, Barclay works No. 880 of 1900, is seen shunting in early preservation days at Market Overton in September 1975. (David Ford)

The final Barclay crane was an order from Tata Ltd for an unusual 0-6-2, works No. 2231 of 1947, destined for an Indian steelworks.

during the First World War. The next locomotive, works No. 213, a product of 1893, went to another steelworks, this time the Lanarkshire Steel Company at Motherwell; the third, dating from 1917, was another order from Glengarnock.

Black Hawthorn and Cranes for Consett

The Gateshead firm Black Hawthorn & Company built two cranes based on conventional four-coupled locomotives, but with the crane carried on an extended rear frame, over a four-wheel bogie, resulting in an 0-4-4 wheel arrangement. The centre post of the crane was mounted directly above the central pin of the bogie.

The first of these two machines was delivered in 1876 to John Spencer & Sons for use in their Newburn steelworks. It was of standard gauge, with 10-inch-diameter x 17-inch-stroke cylinders, with coupled wheels of only 2-foot 8-inch diameter and bogie wheels of 1-foot 6-inch diameter. The bogie was allowed a generous lateral sideplay of 12 inches, which allowed the locomotive to negotiate very tight curves, even with an overall wheelbase of 16 feet. The overall length of the locomotive was 29 feet 7 inches, and the total weight was 24 tons.

The crane, with wrought-iron jib and cast-iron bed plate was designed to allow a 4-ton lift, with a jib radius of 9 feet. The lifting mechanism of the crane was steam powered, but the slewing function had to be carried out by hand. The Newburn steelworks continued in operation until 1928 when the locomotive was sold to T. W. Ward.

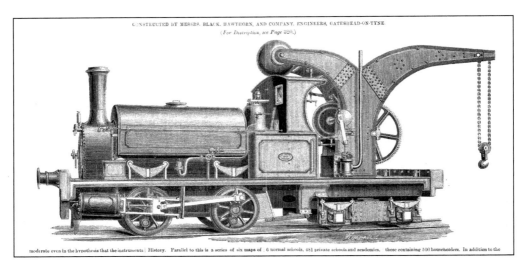

The first 0-4-4 crane tank by Black Hawthorn, works No. 358 of 1876.

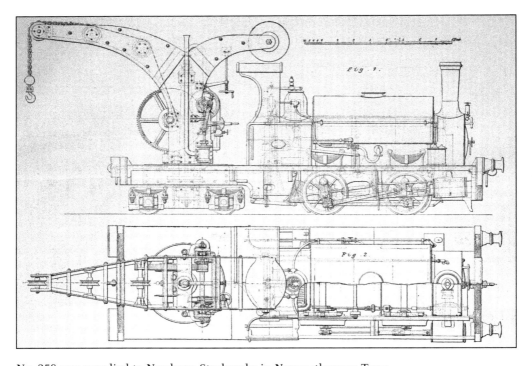

No. 358 was supplied to Newburn Steelworks in Newcastle-upon-Tyne.

The second such crane locomotive was constructed in 1895 to metre gauge for the Wallsend-on-Tyne shipyard of Swan Hunter. A smaller machine, it was fitted with 7¼ inch x 12-inch cylinders and 2-foot-diameter coupled wheels. At around this time the company was advertising, 'Crane locomotives for steelworks, from 2 to 12 tons capacity.'

Metre-gauge Black Hawthorn No. 1117 of 1895 was still working with Swan Hunter in 1956. (RCTS Archive, Jack Faithfull collection)

However, in 1885 Messrs Black Hawthorn had built an 0-4-0 vertical-boilered crane locomotive, works No. 831, for the Consett Iron Company. Resembling a locomotive crane but with outside cylinders of 8-inch diameter and 12-inch stroke, driving wheels of 2-foot 9-inch diameter and a rated lifting capacity of 2 tons, the machine was the first of eight designed specifically for the Consett company.

The second order, placed in January 1887, was for two much heavier cranes, each with a 12-ton lift, carried on a locomotive chassis with a 2-4-0 wheel arrangement. With works Nos 897/8, they had 13½ x 21-inch outside cylinders and 3-foot-diameter driving wheels.

The remaining five Consett cranes, plus two more ordered in 1889 by the Dowlais Iron Company in Cardiff, were all rated at 7 tons, with 12-inch-diameter by 21½-inch-stroke cylinders and 3-foot-diameter driving wheels. One was ordered in 1888, with three more in 1891. The last one, which carried works No. 1206, was actually ordered in December 1900, after the Black Hawthorn business had been taken over by the partnership Chapman & Furneaux in 1896. This entity continued in business until 1902 when the goodwill passed to R&W Hawthorn Leslie & Company, which built E No. 13, works No. 2984 of 1913, which carried the name *Rose*.

Black Hawthorn was not the only supplier to the Consett Iron Company. In 1897, Robert Stephenson & Company built an 0-4-0 vertical boiler crane locomotive at its Newcastle works, No. 2853, followed a year later by No. 2854, this time with a 2-4-0 wheel arrangement. They were subsequently numbered E No. 8 and E No. 9 by the Consett works.

Consett Steelworks operated a number of vertical-boilered crane locomotives, including several by Black Hawthorn, of which E No. 1 was the last to be withdrawn, passing to Beamish Museum for preservation. (Jonathan Marsh)

Clarke Chapman also supplied two 0-4-0 7-ton cranes to Consett in 1907, one of which survived until 1968. (Clarke Chapman)

Another local Gateshead firm, but this time a specialist crane maker rather than locomotive builder, Clarke Chapman & Company built two very similar 0-4-0 vertical-boilered crane locomotives at its Victoria Works in 1907. With works Nos 7519 and 7520, they were numbered E No. 11 and E No. 12 by the Consett operator. Designed for a lifting capacity of 7 tons, they remained at work until 1953 and 1968 respectively.

Finally, the Motherwell-based crane maker Marshall Fleming & Company, established in 1890, had produced its first locomotive cranes six years later. In 1921, they built three 0-4-0 outside-cylindered, vertical-boilered crane locomotives for Consett, which were numbered E Nos 15–17, one of which disgraced itself with a boiler explosion in later life.

E No. 1, one of the Black Hawthorn 2-4-0 examples, was still at work into the late 1970s, by that time converted to oil firing, and is believed to have been the last crane locomotive at work in the UK. It survives in the care of Beamish Museum.

The Consett company also operated several 'conventional' crane locomotives built by Dübs and Andrew Barclay, plus a large fleet of vertical-boilered locomotive cranes.

Further south, Stothert & Pitt, of Bath, built a number of 15-ton vertical-boilered crane locomotives, but with the outside cylinders driving just one axle, resulting in a 2-2-0 wheel arrangement. Customers included the Landore Siemens Steel Company in South Wales and Bolckow Vaughan & Company on Teesside in 1891. The well-known, Leeds-based

An eight-coupled, vertical-boilered crane locomotive was built for the Buenos Aries Western Railway Argentina by Thomas Smith of Rodley in 1910. (Matias Chiodini)

crane maker Thomas Smith & Sons (Rodley) built at least one eight-coupled 5-ton crane locomotive in 1910 for the Buenos Aries Western Railway, which has survived in preservation in Argentina.

On the Continent, the state-owned Belgian company John Cockerill built a number of outside-cylindered, vertical-boilered crane locomotives, some of which served as coaling cranes at railway sheds. The company, named after its British-born founder, had many interests from iron and steel production to large stationary and marine steam engines, plus locomotive construction. Designs for small, vertical-boilered shunting/light railway locomotives were particularly successful, and the crane locomotives were based around these chassis. At least two were eventually acquired by heritage railways, including the former coaling crane from Schaerbeek locomotive depot, which was based on a stretched Type 4 locomotive chassis. This spent several years at Maldegem Steam Centre, but was scrapped in 2017 as it was incomplete and in poor condition.

Belgian State Railways used several Cockerill crane locomotives for coaling. This example was sold for possible preservation at Maldegem, but was scrapped in 2017. (Kevin Hoggett)

R&W Hawthorn Leslie

By far the largest builder of crane locomotives was R&W Hawthorn Leslie & Company, which had both locomotive and shipbuilding interests at sites in Newcastle upon Tyne. Over eighty such machines were built at the Forth Banks Works between 1881 and 1950, although the first four were actually built by R&W Hawthorn before its merger with the shipbuilder Andrew Leslie & Company of Hebburn upon Tyne, and the final eight were constructed after the locomotive building side of the business was taken over by Robert Stephenson in 1937 to become Robert Stephenson & Hawthorns. As shipbuilders, the Hawthorn Leslie name continued until subsumed into British Shipbuilders in 1977.

Hawthorn Leslie adopted a rather novel approach to its standard design of crane locomotive, with the crane mounted directly over the firebox, which was circular on plan and extended in height. The lifting function was unconventional in that the crane was not fitted with a separate hoisting engine operating cables and drum, but the jib was fitted with fixed hooks, at various radii, and lifted by means of a piston, acting as a lever, located within the boiler space over the firebox. A two-cylinder engine linked by gearing to a toothed ring around the top of the circular firebox extension operated the slewing function. The lifting function was controlled by varying steam pressure to the underside of the piston – the upper side of which was constantly subject to boiler pressure. Thus, by exhausting steam to the underside the pressure on top would create lift and, building

R&W Hawthorn No. 1979 of 1884, a 2-ton crane built before the merger to form Hawthorn Leslie. (South Tyneside Libraries collection)

pressure on the underside to equilibrium together with the weight of the jib, would lower the load. The locomotive design incorporated a modified Joy valve gear.

The first crane locomotive, works No. 1863, emerged in 1881 for Charles Mitchell & Company's shipyard at Low Walker, where it was christened *Jumbo*. This was a relatively small machine with cylinders of only 9-inch diameter and 14-inch stroke, and wheels of 2-foot 4-inch diameter. There then followed an order from the shipbuilders Denny of Dumbarton for a crane with 10 x 15-inch cylinders and 2-foot 9-inch-diameter wheels, works No. 1877, which was reputedly a well tank, rather than the usual side tank, named *Leven*.

The shipbuilders Charles Mitchell & Company merged with WG Armstrong to become Armstrong Mitchell & Company in 1885, and this new company took delivery of works No. 1979 that year, with two more, Nos 2047/8, in 1886. Meanwhile, another crane tank had been completed for the Royal Italian Government Railways. All the cranes built thus far were rated at a maximum capacity of 4-tons.

In 1887, the Australian city of Adelaide hosted the Jubilee Exhibition – the event marking the fiftieth anniversary of the accession of Queen Victoria to the throne – and Hawthorn Leslie exhibited works No. 2075, a 3-foot 6-inch-gauge locomotive with a 2-ton-capacity crane, which was supplied to the railway contractor Edward Keane. Named *Renown*, it was engaged on the construction of the Midland Railway in Western Australia, before passing, with crane removed, to MC Davies, a timber contractor. This was followed in 1888 by a 4-ton crane, works No. 2083, for Stockton Iron Company, which named it *Stephenson*.

The distinctive design and method of crane mounting is clearly shown in this view of Hawthorn Leslie works No. 2048, built in 1886 and initially named *Jubilee* in honour of the event of the following year. (Alon Siton)

The second crane tank built in 1888 was something of an oddity. William Cross, who worked for the company, took out a patent, No. 14,770, for a hydraulic crane locomotive. The patent specification depicted a locomotive with a 2-2-2 wheel arrangement and the centre point of the crane almost directly above the single driving axle, the crane structure mounted on an arched frame over the boiler, supported by the side tanks. The steam-driven pumps used water from the main tanks, rather than a separate fluid, in the hydraulic systems of the lifting and turning rams. The slewing function utilised opposing rams linked by a chain.

As built, the locomotive, works No. 2113 featured outside frames and, again, unusually, inside cylinders, with dimensions of 14-inch diameter and 18-inch stroke. The crane jib, bearing the legend 'Cross Patent', was of steel plate construction and was capable of a maximum lift of 10 tons. The completed machine was supplied to the Jarrow shipyard and steelworks of Palmers Shipbuilding & Iron Company. This concern took another standard pattern crane tank, No. 2447 in 1900, which it named *Hector,* and later acquired *Leven* from Denny of Dumbarton. For a time, it also operated *Egbert,* No. 2173 of 1890, which later went to Robert Stephenson to be converted to a more conventional saddle tank locomotive. The Jarrow yard suffered greatly in the depression of the early 1930, with the last ship launched in 1932, and within three years the whole site had been demolished.

A unique locomotive built at the Forth Banks works was the Cross Patent hydraulic crane, works No. 2113 of 1888, which was supplied to the local shipbuilder Palmers. (South Tyneside Libraries collection)

A works photograph demonstrating the capabilities of the cross-hydraulic crane. (South Tyneside Libraries collection)

Forth Banks Works continued to turn out the now familiar style of crane locomotive, with a 4-ton example, No. 2137 of 1889, destined for Armstrong Mitchell, appropriately named *Giraffe*, followed by *Camel* in 1896. A second locomotive named *Camel* was delivered to Vickers, Sons & Maxim in 1898, a company with shipbuilding interests in Barrow-in-Furness, plus other engineering works in Sheffield, Erith and Dartford. A second order, named *Dromedary*, followed a year later. Armstrong Mitchell merged with Joseph Whitworth & Company to form WG Armstrong, Whitworth & Company in the following year, and the new concern subsequently bought five more. The first of these was named *Openshaw* when delivered in 1899, and *Jesmond* followed the following year. *Lion* joined the fleet in 1902, with *Bear* added in 1906 and *Hawthorn* in 1910.

The British Admiralty ordered no less than nine examples between 1890 and 1938, with the first destined for Pembroke Dockyard, plus four for Portsmouth, built in 1895, 1899, 1904 and 1938, which it numbered 7, 8, 1 and 12 respectively. A second for Pembroke in 1901 was named *Nelson*, and Chatham Dockyard chose the name *Hercules* for theirs in 1909, but Devonport and Sheerness merely gave theirs the Nos 6 and 100 respectively in 1904.

The Dutch-owned shipbuilding company Koninklyke Scheepsbouw Maatschapij, with extensive interests in the Dutch East Indies, now Indonesia, ordered a crane in 1895, which it named *Willy* and employed in its De Schelde Vlissingen shipyard until withdrawal in 1929. John Birch & Company, a London-based contractor and agent for railway equipment,

60

An 1891 works photograph of works No. 2227, demonstrating the lifting capacity of the crane. This was supplied to Armstrong Whitworth & Co., where it was named *Gabrielle*.

Hawthorn Leslie works No. 2768 of 1910 was a heavier, 7-ton-capacity crane built for Sir W. G. Armstrong Whitworth & Co. (W. Embleton)

ordered a crane in 1904, which was destined for Russia and named *COPMOBO*. Other export orders came in 1908/9 from Takata, Japan Steelworks and Stewart & Grey (Trieste), while works No. 2783 was exhibited at a Brussels Trade Fair in 1910, and in 1924 works No. 3583 was displayed closer to home at the Wembley Empire exhibition. The mining company Rio Tinto bought two 3-foot 6-inch-gauge cranes – the first in 1913, the second following in 1930 as its No. 150 – which the company has preserved at its own museum at Huelva in Spain. The iron and steel works of William Sandford bought works No. 2605 in 1905 for its Eskbank works in Australia. Appropriately named *Eskbank*, it was joined in 1909 by *Shifter*, a similar crane, No. 2403, which had been built in 1898 for the Patent Shaft & Axletree Company of Wednesbury, Staffordshire. Both were later transferred to Port Kembla Steelworks and scrapped in February 1938.

Virtually all orders for the domestic market were placed by iron and steel works or companies with shipbuilding interests. One exception was an order for a crane tank, works No. 2446, built for Birmingham Railway Carriage & Wagon Company, while rather more unusually the Carlisle firm Carr & Co., a prominent biscuit manufacturer, bought works No. 2669, which it named *Dispatch*, in 1907. Other companies which placed orders for a single locomotive in the Edwardian period included Central Marine Engine Works at Hartlepool, Fownes Forge & Engineering Company, Cochrane & Co., Middlesbrough,

Works No. 3035 of 1914 was one of a pair a 7-ton cranes ordered by New South Wales Government Railways as its No. Lo 11. It is seen here at Eveleigh before renumbering as 1052 in 1924. In 1978, it was sold to the Dorrigo Railway Museum. (University of Newcastle)

A 1926 view of Lithgow Ironworks, with *Eskbank*, works No. 2606, standing beside the weighbridge. (Lithgow Library)

On display at the Rio Tinto Museum at Huelva in Spain is works No. 3785, a 3-foot 6-inch-gauge product of 1930. (Rio Tinto Museum)

Scotts Shipbuilding & Engineering Co., and Cammell Laird at Birkenhead. The Norfolk Steelworks of Thomas Firth & Sons at Sheffield bought one, as did the gas plant engineers Ashmore, Benson, Pease & Co., which named its crane tank *Parkfield* after its works in Stockton. From 1900 another, bearing the name *Haskin*, could be found at work at the Northern Wood Haskinising Company at Newcastle, until it passed to the Albert Hill Foundry of Thomas Summersons & Sons at Darlington, a firm engaged in the manufacture of railway track, points and other associated equipment, and which renamed it *Herald*.

In 1913 the company produced the first two of four six-coupled crane tanks, No.2957, built to 5-foot 6-inch gauge for Ceylon Government Railways as its No. 163, and No. 2982 for Sampaio Correa & Company of Brazil – a client that also ordered another, standard pattern crane, No. 2983, at the same time, numbering them 1 and 2 respectively. The third six-coupled tank was No. 3538 of 1922 for the Great Indian Peninsular Railways, which allocated it the No. 3, and this is preserved at the National Railway Museum in Delhi. The fourth example was No. 3690 of 1927 for the Great Northern Railway of Ireland, as its No. 31. All four had 14-inch diameter x 20-inch-stroke cylinders with Walschaert's valve gear, 3-foot 4-inch-diameter wheels, and a crane with a maximum capacity of 9 tons.

Six locomotives were completed in 1902, two of which were ordered by William Doxford & Sons, and these were the first members of what would eventually become one of the best-known fleets of crane tanks. These were Nos 2517 and 2535, which were named

Two cranes were built for the Central Railway of Brazil in 1913. Works No. 2982 was of 5-foot 3-inch gauge. (South Tyneside Libraries collection)

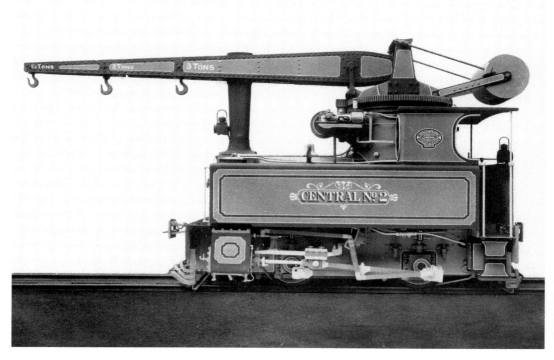

The second crane for the Central Railway was a 2-ton example, built for the metre-gauge network. (South Tyneside Libraries collection)

Another example of four six-coupled cranes by Hawthorn Leslie, works No. 3538 of 1922 was built for the Great Indian Peninsular Railway. (South Tyneside Libraries collection)

Pallion and *Deptford* respectively by the Sunderland shipyard. The shipyard railway system operated on three separate levels, with steeply graded zig-zag connections between them to accommodate a total difference in height of nearly 100 feet, plus a mainline connection. Works No. 2551 *Wear* followed a year later with No. 2594 *Hylton* joining the operation in 1906, and No. 2632 *Millfield* added in 1908. No. 2550 of 1903, with the name *Brownie*, was destined for the Hawthorn Leslie shipyard at Hebburn, but that too eventually went to Doxford's in 1940, two years after *Millfield* was withdrawn and scrapped. For many years the engines were kept in a shed, each allocated its own space, with its name painted on the entrance doors. During the Second World War Doxford was struggling to keep up with wartime demands for shipping tonnage and ordered four more crane tanks – two of which were delivered in 1940 and the second pair in 1942. However, to continue the Doxford story we must return to 1917, a year that the New Russia Company placed an order for two crane locomotives. The order was allocated works Nos 3327 and 3328, and many components were made. However, it was also the year of the Russian Revolution, and inevitably the order was cancelled, with all the parts being placed in store.

By the time the next Doxford order was placed Hawthorn Leslie had become part of Robert Stephenson & Hawthorns, but, allocated new works Nos of 7006 and 7007, the two new builds of 1940 incorporated the parts set aside over twenty years earlier. Named *Roker* and *Hendon* by the new owner, continuing the practice of naming after areas of Sunderland, they were joined two years later by Nos 7069 and 7070, which became

The Doxford shipyard in Sunderland became well known for its fleet of crane tanks in later years. In this 1928 view engines and some of their crew pose outside the shed. Note the locomotive names painted on the shed doors. (Tyne & Wear Archives)

By 1968 the shed had lost its doors and most of the roof. Four crane tanks plus the yard's only conventional locomotive, *General*, await their next duties in May 1967. (Leslie Pitcher)

Millfield waits with a wagon loaded with steel plate while the crew struggle to clear an obstruction with a point mechanism. (Jonathan Marsh)

Southwick's crane in use sorting steel sections at the Doxford shipyard in 1969. (Jonathan Marsh)

RSH works No. 7070 of 1942, *Millfield*, trundles through the yard with a wagon-load of plate. (Jonathan Marsh)

Roker rests at the coal stage in the shed yard, while crews take their lunch break. (Jonathan Marsh)

Lunch break over and the engines are prepared for their next tasks, as epitomised in this 1969 scene. (Jonathan Marsh)

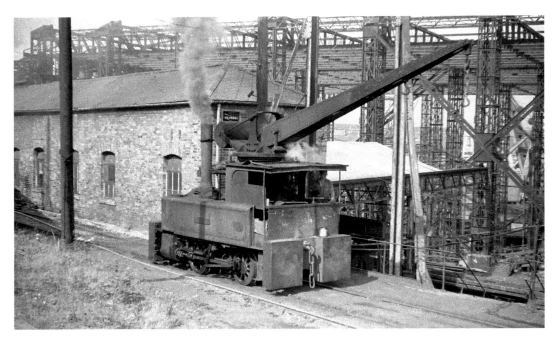

Against the unmistakeable backdrop of shipyard architecture, *Roker*, RSH works No. 7007 of 1940, prepares for the next job. (Jonathan Marsh)

A gang of 'slingers' assist an unidentified Robert Stephenson & Hawthorn crane tank loading wagons at the Doxford shipyard, Sunderland, *c.* 1968. (Alan Murray Rust)

Above: The boiler from *Southwick*, built by RSH in 1942, removed for overhaul, showing the crane-operating piston rod and cover over the firebox. (Bahamas Locomotive Society)

Right: The 1903-built *Brownie* is tucked away in an archway of the bridge behind the main Doxford shed in May 1967. (Leslie Pitcher)

The partially dismantled remains of *Grindon* and *Brownie* at Doxford in October 1968. (David Glenn)

Southwick and the replacement *Millfield* respectively. The crane tanks were joined by one conventional locomotive, a Peckett saddle tank dating from 1944 and named *General*, which operated to and from the exchange sidings, while another non-standard addition to the fleet was *Grindon*, a product of Andrew Barclay in 1912. At least three Doxford locomotives spent their last years working with cranes removed, and *Deptford, Wear* and *Hylton* had been scrapped by late 1952. *Grindon* and *Brownie* followed in 1969, but the railway within the shipyard continued, with the crane tanks affectionately known by local residents as 'Elephants', until February 1971 when the remaining locomotives were withdrawn and sold. By this time they were all practically worn out, but fortunately the four Robert Stephenson & Hawthorns examples have survived. Initially *Pallion* too was privately purchased and, with *Roker*, taken to storage at Middlesbrough, but later scrapped. *Hendon*, which is now in the care of the Tanfield Railway, was actually purchased from a scrap merchant, Blaydon Metals, in 1974, and *Roker* is also appropriately displayed nearby at Beamish Museum.

Only one other crane tank was constructed during the war years, works No. 7126, delivered in 1943 to the Hawthorn Leslie shipyard at Hebburn.

The last two crane locomotives to be constructed at the Forth Banks Works, and in fact the last such built in Britain, were works Nos 7542 and 7543, for the New South Wales Government Railways in 1950 as its Nos 1080 and 1083. These were heavier machines, each with 14-inch-diameter and 20-inch-stroke cylinders, with 3-foot 3-inch-diameter wheels and a 7-ton capacity crane. NSWGR had previously bought others from Hawthorn Leslie, with the first two, Nos 3034/5 supplied in 1914 as its numbers Lo 10 and Lo 11. Four more followed between 1923 and 1925, works Nos 3563/4/5 and 3635, with Australian numbers

The last crane locomotive to be built in Britain was Robert Stephenson & Hawthorns works No. 7543, one of a pair supplied to New South Wales Government Railways in 1950. No. 1083 is preserved at the former Eveleigh workshops site.

Lo 40 / 1 and Lo 47 / 8. The NSWGR subsequently renumbered the earlier engines into its miscellaneous X10 class, with them becoming Nos 1051/2 and 1066–9 respectively. They worked in various workshops around the system, such as Eveleigh, Cardiff, Chulloa and the Clyde Wagon Works. Although mainline steam officially ended in 1973 it is known that several of the crane tanks were at work well beyond this date. Remarkably, one was undergoing overhaul at Eveleigh as late as 1980, but it would appear that this work was carried out almost furtively, as if to hide it from senior management. Remarkably, five have been preserved: three (Nos 1052 and 1067/8) at the Dorrigo Steam Railway, one (No. 1082) at the Sydney Powerhouse Museum and one (No. 1083) at the Eveleigh Technology Park. No. 1067, now at Dorrigo, was dismantled in the 1970s for an overhaul that did not go ahead, and has remained in that condition since.

Beyer Peacock

Between 1855 and 1958 the firm of Beyer Peacock built nearly 8,000 locomotives, with many destined for export, but only a handful were crane locomotives.

The first was actually an 0-4-0 saddle tank, works No. 1827, turned out in 1879 for the company's own use as a yard shunter at its Gorton Foundry works in Manchester. Six years later it was fitted with a pair of trailing wheels and a rear-mounted crane, thus becoming an 0-4-2CT. It served in this form until removal of the crane and trailing axle in 1945. It continued in service at Gorton, but when the works closed in 1966, it was sold and mounted on a plinth near Wilmslow, Cheshire. In 1973, it was sold again and moved to the fledgeling Cambrian Railway preservation project at Oswestry, but eventually finding a home at the Foxfield Railway in Staffordshire, where it has been restored and returned to steam.

In 1891, a very similar, but purpose-built, 0-4-2 crane tank, works No. 3343, was built to 5-foot 6-inch gauge for the Buenos Aires & Rosario Railway in Argentina. The locomotive was fitted with a half-type cab, but the rear-mounted crane also had a separate canopy. With 12-inch diameter x 18-inch-stroke cylinders, it had 3-foot-diameter driving wheels.

The next crane order was for two six-coupled locomotives, to 3-foot 6-inch gauge, works Nos 4317/8 for Queensland Government Railways delivered in 1902. Once again these were saddle tanks with a rear-mounted crane, but this time the crane mechanisms were hydraulically operated and the locomotives were also fitted with hydraulic presses, which would lift the locomotive weight off the springs to allow greater stability during crane operation. The hydraulic systems used oil rather than water, as in some other early designs. The jib of one of the cranes was reputedly lost overboard in a storm during the voyage to Australia. The cranes were removed in 1912 and both locomotives withdrawn in 1927.

The first crane locomotive built by Beyer Peacock was works No. 1827 of 1879. Although built as a conventional saddle tank, it was converted with a crane in 1885 and served the company as the Gorton works shunter for many years.

The crane from Beyer Peacock 1827 of 1879 was removed in its last years of service, but it is now preserved at the Foxfield Railway. (John Allman)

In 1902, Beyer Peacock built two locomotives with 3-ton cranes, works Nos 4317/8 for the 3-foot 6-inch-gauge Queensland Railways. Both had been withdrawn by 1927. (Chris Drymalik)

The Buenos Aires & Rosario Railway ordered two more crane locomotives, which were completed in 1908, works Nos 5000/1. As before, they were 5-foot 6-inch gauge, six-coupled machines, but this time were a heavier design with steam-operated cranes, capable of a 5-ton lift at 18-foot radius, mounted centrally over the boiler, which also meant that they were fitted with side tanks rather than a saddle. The boilers featured Belpaire fireboxes, Walschaert's valve gear was fitted, and the complete locomotive in working order weighed in at 45½ tons. The crane controls were duplicated, with one set each side of the footplate for convenience of operation.

The final order was for two cranes for New South Wales Government Railways in 1909. These were standard-gauge 0-4-2 side tanks, with rear-mounted 5-ton-capacity cranes, works Nos 5260/1, which also featured Belpaire fireboxes and Walschaert's valve gear with 3-foot 3-inch-diameter coupled wheels. They were initially numbered Lo 5/Lo 6 and allocated to Honeysuckle Works, but became 1046/7 after the 1924 renumbering scheme and continued at work until they were both scrapped in 1968.

Another Manchester-based firm, which built just one crane locomotive for its own yard use, was Nasmyth, Wilson & Company of the Bridgewater Foundry, Patricroft. As Nasmyth & Gaskell, the first locomotives had been constructed as early as 1839, and over the ensuing century some 1, 650 were produced in total, of which over 1,000 were exported. Works No. 1268 was an 0-6-0 side tank crane locomotive built in 1921 for yard duties. Appropriately named *James Nasmyth*, it had 3-foot-diameter driving wheels and cylinders of 13-inch diameter and 22-inch stroke.

Two 0-4-2 crane tanks were ordered by New South Wales Government Railways and completed by the Gorton Works in 1909. With works Nos 5620/1, they were originally numbered Lo 05/6, but were renumbered 1046/7 in 1924. Both were withdrawn in 1968. (Chris Drymalik)

NSWGR No. 1047 is seen here towards the end of its working life at the Honeysuckle permanent way works in Newcastle.

Vulcan Foundry

The origins of the Vulcan Foundry at Newton-le-Willows can be traced back to 1830 when Charles Tayleur set up a foundry business as Charles Tayleur & Company, with Robert Stephenson joining as a partner two years later. Stephenson later bowed out because of other commitments, but the firm established itself with, among other projects, the supply of ironwork to the fledgling Liverpool & Manchester Railway. Orders for locomotives followed and in 1842 Henry Dübs, who we encountered earlier, became works manager, and five years later the company name was changed to the Vulcan Foundry Company.

Although a prolific locomotive builder, Vulcan Foundry only produced eleven crane locomotives between 1895 and 1911. The first, which formed part of an army contract, was an 0-6-0 side tank, works No. 1435, and named *Shoeburyness*, with 3-foot 3-inch-diameter driving wheels, 16-inch diameter x 20-inch-stroke outside cylinders and Walschaert's valve gear. Most unusually, it was fitted with not one but two 5-ton cranes, one mounted each side of the locomotive in a false bunker, with mounting framework that extended below the running plate. The 'bunker' side panels could be opened out to permit operation of the cranes, which could apparently be stored behind folding rear cab panels when not in use. With the cranes stowed out of use it would have virtually presented an appearance of a normal locomotive.

Such a design only allowed a very limited slewing arc and was presumably intended for a very specific purpose at the Shoeburyness army ranges, but the locomotive spent the later part of its working life at Chatham Dockyard, although its final disposal date and fate are not known.

The second crane tank was an 0-4-2 saddle tank, built in 1902 for the company's own yard use. Works No. 1828 and named *Bee*, it had a rear-mounted crane rated at 4 tons. Although the crane had a steam hoisting engine, slewing was carried by hand with a rope attached to the jib, although the Vulcan works catalogue advised that steam operation could be specified.

All subsequent crane locomotives were export orders, with the next for West Australian Government Railways. This was works No. 1897 of 1903, an 0-6-2 side tank built to 3-foot 6-inch gauge with a 3-ton rear-mounted crane. It was the sole member of the WAGR U7 class and was originally purchased for a pipe-laying project, but was subsequently employed at the Midland Railway workshops. In 1925, the crane was removed and, with increased coal and water capacity (it was delivered with 600 gallons water capacity while the bunker could accommodate 1½ tons of coal), it entered service as a normal locomotive until withdrawn and scrapped in 1940. Principal dimensions were cylinders 14 inches in diameter and 20-inch stroke with 3-foot-diameter wheels and a 12-foot wheelbase.

The remainder all went to India, with works No. 2156 following in 1906 for the Oudh & Rohilkund Railway in northern India for use as a yard shunter at Alambagh, Lucknow. This was an 0-4-2 side tank, built to 5-foot 6-inch gauge, with a 6-ton-capacity rear-mounted crane. An order for two very similar locomotives, works Nos 2421/2 was completed in 1906 for the North Western State Railway, with works No. 3120 following in 1911, also built to the broad gauge, for the Bengal Nagpur Railway.

Vulcan Foundry works No. 1436 of 1894 *Shoeburyness* was originally supplied to the Shoeburyness Naval Tramway and later transferred to Chatham Dockyard. Unusually specified with two cranes, only one is visible in this view. (Dockyard Railway)

In 1902, Vulcan Foundry built an 0-4-2 saddle tank, works No. 1828, with a 4-ton crane, named *Bee*, for its own yard use. (P. Stratford)

Vulcan Foundry works No. 1897 of 1903 was ordered by West Australian Government Railways for a pipe-laying project. It was the sole member of the railway's U7 class.

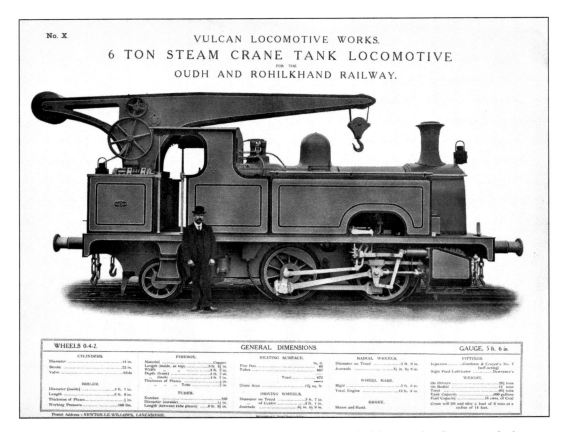

The 5-foot 6-inch-gauge Oudh & Rohikund Railway in India took delivery of Vulcan Foundry's works No 2156 in 1906 for use at Alambagh, Lucknow. (Alon Siton)

The Great India Peninsular Railway, which had been founded in London in 1849, was the destination of Nos 3131 and 3132, while two more, Nos 3133 and 3134, went to the Eastern Bengal Railway. All four locomotives were similar six-coupled side tanks, once again built for 5-foot 6-inch gauge with rear-mounted cranes, completed in 1915.

The Bengal cranes had a maximum lift of 6 tons at 14-foot radius, while the Peninsular machines were rated at 4½ tons at 16-foot radius. All were outside cylindered with Walschaert's valve gear and, while they shared a wheel diameter of 3 feet 7 inches, the wheelbase of the Bengal engines was 13 feet 6 inches – 1 foot shorter than the other pair. However, with a weight in working order of 45½ tons, they were 1½ tons heavier.

In addition to these purpose-built crane locomotives, Vulcan Foundry had fitted a crane to an existing locomotive for the Great Central Railway in 1903 as described earlier.

Manning Wardle

Of the 2,000 or so locomotives built at the Boyne Engine Works in Leeds by Manning Wardle, a company that largely supplied contractors and industrial railways, just four were crane tanks. In each case the cranes and mechanisms were supplied by the local specialist maker, Joseph Booth & Brothers, Rodley.

The first, works No. 578, was a four-coupled side tank supplied in June 1875 to local customer Kirkstall Forge, an engineering firm that could trace its roots back to the twelfth century and the monks of Kirkstall Abbey. At the time of the locomotive's purchase, the company was able to offer a wide range of products, from railway axles and wheels to heavy forge presses and even its own complete rail-mounted, self-propelled steam cranes. However, after only nine years use, the crane was removed from the Manning Wardle tank in 1884.

Nearly thirty years elapsed before the next crane locomotive was built, an 0-6-0 side tank, works No. 1612 of 1903, to 5-foot 6-inch gauge destined for India.

In 1913, a four-coupled crane locomotive, works No. 1811, built to 3-foot 6-inch gauge, was supplied to the Victoria Falls and Transvaal Power Company in South Africa. This engine had 3-foot 6-inch-diameter wheels and 14-inch diameter x 20-inch-stroke outside cylinders, with a 2-ton capacity crane. While all the other locomotives in the company's varied fleet carried names, this one was simply known as *Crane*. It was set to work at the Vereeniging Power Station where it was employed until withdrawn and scrapped in 1936. Initially it was used in the construction of the power station, but subsequently to haul coal trains from the mainline to the plant – a distance of around two-thirds of a mile. The crane was reportedly removed after the end of the construction period. From 1925 the Manning

The first crane built by Manning Wardle was works No. 578 for Kirkstall Forge in 1875. (Mark Smithers)

Wardle worked alongside another locomotive that had originally been built as a crane tank. Named *Volta*, it was a product of J. A. Maffei in Munich, works No. 2468, in 1904. It was supplied to Rand Central Electric Works for use at Brakpan Power Station where it stayed until 1913 when transferred to Rosherville, and thence to Vereeniging. It was subsequently sold for use at Orlando Power Station in Johannesburg. Adjacent to the Vereeniging site was the Union Steel Corporation, which employed Andrew Barclay crane tank No. 1426 of 1916 until it was scrapped in 1950.

The last of the four Manning Wardle cranes was delivered in February 1918 to Thomas Firth & Company in Sheffield for use at its steelworks. This four-coupled outside-cylindered engine carried a 3-ton-capacity crane.

Also based in Leeds was the locomotive building firm of Hudswell, Clarke & Company. Like its near neighbour Manning Wardle, of the 1,800 or so locomotives produced over a century of manufacture only four were fitted with cranes, and these appeared over a twelve-year period from 1911 to 1923. Again, like Manning Wardle, it bought in crane equipment from a specialist maker, but this time using two local suppliers, Joseph Booth and its nearby competitor Thomas Smith & Sons.

The first, allocated works No. 945, was ordered by the Partington Steel & Iron Company of Irlam Works, Manchester, in 1911. It was a four-coupled outside-cylindered side tank with a crane by Thomas Smith & Sons, rated for a 5-ton capacity lift at a radius of 15 feet. Complete with ballast it weighed 40¾ tons.

The next two crane locomotives were destined for Australia. Works No. 1025, ordered by Commonwealth Railways, was the first of these and was shipped to Fremantle in 1913. Broadly similar in design to the predecessor, it was, however, fitted with a crane by Joseph Booth.

The first crane locomotive built by Hudswell Clarke was works No. 945, supplied in 1911 to Partington Iron & Steel Company. (Alon Siton)

Hudswell Clarke supplied works No. 1025 to Commonwealth Railways of Australia in 1913. Crane No. 1 is seen shunting at Port Augusta in August 1952. (National Railway Museum, Port Adelaide)

A six-coupled locomotive, works No. 1203, followed in 1919, built to a gauge of 5 feet 3 inches for Victoria Government Railways. Joseph Booth again supplied the crane, which in this instance was rated for a 7-ton lift at 14-foot radius. It weighed 46½ tons in working order and had 14-inch diameter x 20-inch-stroke outside cylinders driving coupled wheels of 3 feet 3½ inches in diameter.

The Rivet, Bolt & Nut Company, formerly known as James Millar, of Stobcross Works of Coatbridge was the delivery address for the final order, works No. 1493, in 1923. This was a four-coupled locomotive, with 12-inch diameter and 18-inch-stroke cylinders, but this time with Walschaert's valve gear driving 3-foot 1-inch-diameter wheels. The crane came from Thomas Smith, and was rated for a lift of 2 tons at a radius of 20 feet 6 inches.

Two other well-known Leeds locomotive builders, Kitson & Company and Hunslet Engine Company, are both understood to have prepared crane locomotive designs, although none were actually constructed.

Victoria Railways No. 11 was a Hudswell Clarke product of 1919, with a 7-ton crane. It is seen here shunting at Ballarat North in June 1958. Note the chimney extension. (Wallace Jack, Chris Drymalik collection)

Kerr Stuart

In 1892, Kerr Stuart & Company took over the California Works of Hartley, Arneaux & Fleming at Stoke on Trent. The new company was established by James Kerr, who had a wagon-building business in Glasgow, and his partner John Stuart, and over the ensuing years it built up a reputation formed locomotives intended for both industrial and mainline use.

One particular standard design for an 0-4-0 saddle tank for the basis for a crane locomotive built in 1921. The original design, named *Moss Bay* after the first locomotive built, was adapted by extending the frames forward of the boiler and adding a third, leading, axle, not driven, but of the same 3-foot 3-inch-diameter as the driving wheels. Side tanks of 700-gallon capacity replaced the saddle tank, and the extended frames housed a crane, which was supplied by the specialist crane maker Thomas Smith & Sons (Rodley). This added a further 9 tons to the weight of the locomotive, and the crane itself was capable of lifting 10 tons at a radius of 8 feet or 5 tons at a radius of 16 feet.

This locomotive, of 5-foot 6-inch gauge was built to the order of the Peninsular Locomotive Company of Tatanagar, India. However, this was no ordinary customer, as it was a company, set up in 1921 as a locomotive builder, in which Kerr Stuart held 80 per cent of the capital. Four years later not a single locomotive had been built, and in 1928 the works was taken over by the Indian government and used for the construction of carriage and wagon underframes.

This disastrous investment, compounded by a loan of £78,000 to the fledgling company, led in no small measure to the financial collapse of Kerr Stuart in 1930.

Sentinel

Shrewsbury-based Sentinel Waggon Works built large numbers of vertical-boilered steam waggons, plus geared shunting locomotives and railcars. The London & North Eastern Railway not only bought both railcars and shunters in quantity, but also took delivery of two vertical-boilered crane locomotives – the first in 1929 and the other two years later. The cranes and jibs were supplied by Coles Cranes of Derby, but fitted with Sentinel operating engines. Maximum lifting capacity was 3 tons at a radius of 9 feet, and 1½ tons at a 16-foot. radius. Both spent their lives dealing with locomotive ash at various Scottish sheds. The two cranes were allocated Sentinel works Nos 8157 and 8565, and were initially numbered 773044 and 773066 by the LNER, later becoming 971575/7. No. 773044 was nicknamed *Stoorie Annie* and was employed in Glasgow at both Eastfield and Parkhead sheds, while its sister saw service at Haymarket, St Margaret's, and later Dundee. At times, they had to travel on the running line, and were capable of a speed of 24 miles per hour, with a 50-ton load.

However, when travelling between sheds, No. 773066 apparently had a habit of failing to register its presence on track circuits – a potentially hazardous tendency. In British Railways days they were renumbered in the crane series RS 1032/1½ and RS 1033/1½. (RS denoted Rail Steam, and 1½ the load at maximum radius.) They were withdrawn in July and November 1959 respectively.

Sentinel ash crane RS 1032/1½ is seen at Parkhead shed on 26 July 1953. (RCTS Image Archive, John Young collection)

Cowans Sheldon & Company

Carlisle-based Cowans Sheldon & Company was a specialist crane maker rather than locomotive builder and built up an enviable reputation worldwide as a supplier of heavy railway breakdown cranes. The origins of the firm date back to 1846 when John Cowans, in partnership with Edward Pattison, but also supported by the brothers William and Thomas Bouch established a general engineering works.

While the firm built many self-propelled locomotive cranes, it did supply at least one vertical-boilered, outside-cylindered crane locomotive for the Consett Iron Company – to the same design as the Black Hawthorn machines described earlier.

In 1909, the company built two electric crane locomotives, both of which operated from an overhead power supply, which in itself created restrictions on the potential movement of the crane jib in a potentially hazardous environment. The first of the two locomotives was built for the Glasgow steelworks of F. Braby & Company, but actually ordered and designed by the Glasgow-based consulting engineering firm Spence & Ionides. The crane was capable of lifting 2 tons at a jib radius of 17 feet, and lifting was normally by means of a magnet. The jib was mounted on a 'live' roller ring. The crane could travel at 7 miles per hour by means of two motors, each driving a separate axle. Magnetic brakes were fitted. The Braby crane was built for a two-wire DC power supply, but the second crane, built for the East Indian Railways, was designed for an AC power source.

At around the same time an electric crane locomotive was built by Wolf Maschinefabrik for shunting and loading at its Salbke works, near Magdeburg, in Saxony-Anhalt, Germany. This too used an overhead power supply, and featured an unusual octagonal-shaped cab. A similar machine was built by Saechsische Maschinefabrik, the Chemnitz-based firm originally known by the name of its founder Richard Hartmann, which was used to tow newly completed locomotives through the city streets!

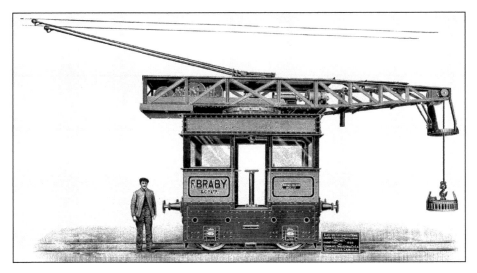

The first of two overhead electric crane locomotives built by Cowans Sheldon in 1908, this particular example was ordered for the Glasgow steelworks of F. Braby.

In 1910, Wolf Maschinefabrik built a similar overhead electric crane for use at its Salbke works, near Magdeburg in Saxony-Anhalt, Germany.

The Third Avenue Railroad of New York built a bogie overhead electric car with a 6-ton-capacity crane supplied by the Whiting Foundry Equipment Company in 1908.

Continental Builders

The vertical-boilered coaling cranes built by Cockerill in Belgium have been discussed previously, but four German manufacturers at least are also known to have to have constructed crane locomotives.

Borsig, a Berlin-based company that became the second largest locomotive builder in the world, outshopped an 0-4-2 crane with a 3-ton lift in 1906, which was displayed at the International Exhibition held that year in Milan. An identical locomotive was supplied to the French State Railway four years later for use at the Sotteville Works near Rouen.

The company also built a fireless crane locomotive in 1928, as did Saechsische Maschinefabrik. Works No. 3841, a standard-gauge machine built in 1915 was supplied to Lange Metallwerke at Aue in Saxony.

In 1912, Jung built its only crane locomotive: an 0-4-2 well tank with outside cylinders and Walschaert's valve gear. The 5-ton-capacity crane was mounted over the boiler on a separate structure fixed to the frames, similar to Barclay and other British designs.

Henschel is known to have built two cranes at its Kassel works: a standard-gauge 0-4-0 with a 2-ton crane and a 750-mm-gauge 0-8-0 for Argentina, while the giant engineering firm Krupp built a four-coupled locomotive with a 3 ton lifting capacity, and a similar design was constructed by Maschinefabrik Esslingen in Baden Württemburg.

In Austria, the Vienna workshops of Maschinefabrik der Staatseisenbahn Gesellschaft built a number of 0-4-2 crane tanks, several of which were supplied to Romanian ironworks at Resita.

Finally, Belgian manufacturer Tubize built two 0-4-2 crane tanks in 1907 and 1928, as its Type 102, for works in Tubize and Nivelles respectively.

Börsig was one of two German manufacturers to construct a fireless crane locomotive.

A more conventional 3-ton crane tank by Börsig.

The only known crane locomotive built by Jüng was works No. 1787 of 1912.

A 3-tonne crane built by Esslingen Maschinefabrik for the Krupp engineering concern.

An eight-coupled, 750-mm-gauge crane tank built in Kassel, Germany, by Henschel in 1922. (Henschel Museum)

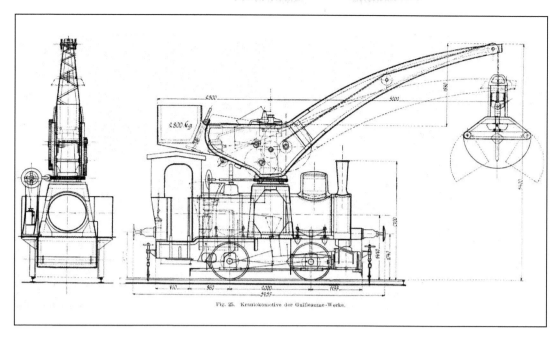

The design for a 2-tonne-capacity crane built by Guilleaume Werke, of Neustadt, near Mannheim.

Built in Vienna, StEG No. 3714 of 1910, this locomotive lost its crane in 1934 but continued to work at a sugar refinery at Siegendorf.

Tubize No. 1928 of 1922, seen at work in the city of its construction. (Luc Delporte)

A rear view of No. 1928 at Tubize. (Luc Delporte)

APPENDIX

Preserved Crane Locomotives

United Kingdom

Number	Works No.	Type	Date Built	Builder	Location
	1827	0-4-0ST	1879	Beyer Peacock	Foxfield Railway (a)
E No. 1	897	2-4-0VBCT	1887	Black Hawthorn	Beamish Museum, ex-Consett Iron Co.
	4101	0-4-0CT	1901	Dübs	Foxfield Railway Ex-Shelton Iron & Steel Co.
1	880	0-4-0CT	1902	Andrew Barclay	Ribble Steam Railway, ex-Glenfield
24	1875	0-4-0CT	1925	Andrew Barclay	Midland Railway Centre, Butterley Ex-Stanton Ironworks
6	2127	0-4-0CT	1942	Andrew Barclay	Bo'ness & Kinneil Railway, ex-Colville
Roker	7006	0-4-0CT	1940	RS&H	Beamish Museum, ex-Doxford
Hendon	7007	0-4-0CT	1940	RS&H	Tanfield Railway, ex-Doxford
Southwick	7069	0-4-0CT	1942	RS&H	Ingrow, Keighley & Worth Valley Railway, ex-Doxford
Millfield	7070	0-4-0CT	1942	RS&H	Private owner, Norfolk, ex-Doxford
Note: a) Crane tank 1885-1945, Gorton works shunter					

Austria

Number	Works No.	Type	Date Built	Builder	Location
Vienna	3714	0-4-2CT	1910	StEG, Vienna	Laufen, Salzkammergut
Note: Static exhibit, preserved minus crane					

Sweden

Number	Works No.	Type	Date Built	Builder	Location
Jumbo	878	0-4-0DM	1900	A. Barclay	Gefle Dala Jernvag Museum, Falun
Note: converted from 0-4-0CT to 0-4-0WT, then to 0-4-0 diesel shunter					

Spain

Number	Works No.	Type	Date Built	Builder	Location
150	3785	0-4-0CT	1930	Hawthorn Leslie	Rio Tinto Museum, Huelva

Argentina

Number	Works No.	Type	Date Built	Builder	Location
C-9	2759	0-4-0CT	1891	Dübs	Ferroclub, Remedios de Escalada
71 V	18087	0-4-0CT	1907	North British	Ferroclub, Haedo
529	7621	0-8-0CT	1910	Smith, Rodley	Ferroclub, Tolosa

India

Number	Works No.	Type	Date Built	Builder	Location
3	3538	0-6-0CT	1922	Hawthorn Leslie	National Railway Museum, Delhi

Australia

	Number	Works No.	Type	Date Built	Builder	Location
New South Wales	1034	2250	0-4-0CT	1886	Dübs	Trainworks, Thirlmere
	1052	3035	0-4-0CT	1914	Hawthorn Leslie	Dorrigo Steam Railway Museum
	1067	3565	0-4-0CT	1924	Hawthorn Leslie	Dorrigo Steam Railway Museum
	1068	3564	0-4-0CT	1924	Hawthorn Leslie	Dorrigo Steam Railway Museum
	1076	995	0-6-0T	1885	Vulcan Foundry	Goulbourn Roundhouse Museum (b)
	1082	7542	0-4-0CT	1950	RS&H	Powerhouse Museum Sydney
	1083	7543	0-4-0CT	1950	RS&H	Technology Park, Eveleigh
All locomotives ex New South Wales Government Railways						
Victoria	2	2711	0-6-0CT	1891	Dübs	ARHS Museum, Melbourne
	Z 526		0-6-0T	1893	Victoria railways	Scienceworks Museum, Melbourne (c)
Both locomotives ex-Victoria Government Railways						
Note: b) Original number R 288, fitted with crane as 0-6-0CT from 1937 to 1959						
Note: c) Built as 0-6-0T, but converted to 0-6-0CT in 1903. Restored to original condition 1983						

Bibliography

Abbott, R. A. S., *Crane Locomotives* (Goose & Son, 1973)

Abbott, R. A. S., *Vertical Boiler Locomotives* (The Oakwood Press, 1989)

Brownlie, John S., *Railway Steam Cranes* (J. S. Brownlie, 1973)

Mountford, Colin and Dave Holroyde, *Industrial Railways and Locomotives of County Durham Part 1* (Industrial Railway Society, 2006)

Tatlow, Peter, *Railway Breakdown Cranes Volume 1* (Noodle Books, 2012)

Tatlow, Peter, *Railway Breakdown Cranes Volume 2* (Noodle Books, 2013)

Tatlow, Peter, *Railway Cranes Volume 3* (Crecy Publishing, 2018)

Acknowledgements

I would firstly like to acknowledge the research carried out by the late Rowland Abbott, and grateful thanks too to David Glenn, plus Chris Drymalik and Ed Slee in Australia, not only for providing illustrations but for their endless patience with my queries.

Many others have kindly provided illustrations, but I would particularly also like to thank John Allman, Leslie Pitcher, Jonathan Marsh and Catrin Galt of South Tyneside Libraries for their help. Photographs not otherwise credited are from the author's collection, and every effort has been made to establish copyright where necessary. However, if we have inadvertently used copyright material without permission/acknowledgement we apologise and we will make the necessary correction at the first opportunity.